Inns and Taverns of Old Arundel

The White Hart.

INNS AND TAVERNS OF OLD ARUNDEL

Rupert Brooks

PHILLIMORE

2009

Published by
PHILLIMORE and CO. LTD
Chichester, West Sussex, England
www.phillimore.co.uk
www.thehistorypress.co.uk

© Rupert Brooks, 2009

ISBN 978-1-86077-606-9

Printed and bound in Great Britain

Dedication

*Dedicated with love and thanks to my wife Margaret Francesca
but for whose unstinting support and forbearance
during the time spent away from her with my research
this book would never have been finished.*

Contents

Preface ... vi

Bibliography ... viii

I   Arundel on the River Arun ... 1

II   Early Taverns and the Emergence of Ale and Beerhouses ... 5

III   Sources of Evidence ... 13

IV   Beerhouses ... 21

V   Alehouses ... 39

VI   Premises without Licence Records ... 77

VII   Conclusions ... 85

Index ... 86

Preface

During the early days of my coming to live in Arundel and becoming fascinated by such a beautiful place and its history, the realisation that little had been written about the people who had made it or of the long-lost places in which they had worked sent me on this quest to write about some of it.

For this a debt of gratitude is owed to all those willing helpers and informants, without whose support, given over several months, many of the memories of Arundel past would have been lost to posterity. Sincere thanks go to my colleagues in Arundel Museum Society, particularly to Pauline Carder for her great encouragement, Eric Nash for allowing me to delve into his collection of the *West Sussex Gazette*, going back to its beginning, and all the books and pamphlets he acquired, and Anthony Pudwell for allowing me access to his own collection of drawings and photographs.

It was my writing in the autumn 2007 issue of *The Bell*, Arundel's own quarterly journal, announcing my intention to research into the history of ale and beerhouses, which brought the first response by telephone from Josie Moseley. Born in 1920, her incredible memory recaptured the atmosphere of Ship Yard and *The Jolly Sailors* and what it was like to live there in those days. Meeting Giles Nullens, who has written on the history of *The Old Ship*, started my research into the publicans who ran the old beerhouses. My need to go to the West Sussex Records Office in Chichester introduced me to Sue Millard and the team of archivists, and they gave me their unstinting help during my endless hours poring over licence records and finding old photographs to go with the text.

Next came contact from Betty Armstrong, whose family tree of the Slaughters showed when earlier generations ran *The Hare and Hounds*, the *General Abercrombie* and *The Ship and Lighter*. On the same family tree was Sandra Pearson, whose grandmother Sylvia Slaughter was born at *The New Inn*, Crossbush, before going to the *Abercrombie*. Other family connections came from Penelope Tryhorn, with her ancestry from the Hulls, and my thanks go to her for her tales and photographs about 'Pegleg' Hulls at *The Jolly Sailors* and Mary Hulls at *The Heart in Hand*.

Talking to residents resulted in first-hand memories of their drinking in many of the ale and beerhouses, the landlords and the layout of the bars. Particular thanks go to Terry Brennan, for recalling details of *The Victory* and *The Old Ship*, and to John Lee for his recollections of both these pubs as well as *The Jolly Sailors*. To be invited to Joan and Gordon Brown's cottage and to be regaled with such detailed reminiscences of *The Railway Inn* was a memorable pleasure. Huge thanks go to Gemma and Ian Odde, the last publican at *The Victory*, for long-lost photographs and their recent memories of the old beerhouse.

Research into the location of the *Bakers Arms* brought me into contact with Margaret and Roger Hodgson, who showed me an early conveyance with conclusive evidence. I then met Sarah Clarke, who had found old coins and tokens above the cellar rubble of cottages in Arun Street, proof enough to give these cottages a beerhouse name. I am indebted for the help given by Ron Kerridge in identifying this find and using his knowledge of old copper coinage, and to Tony Wilson and Tina, now living there, who have encouraged my research and given me their time when proofreading my early drafts.

I am indebted to Margaret Gowler, Ralph Ellis's daughter, for allowing me to include pictures of inn signs painted by her father and for access to notes written by him in the early 1920s.

Enlightenment about the *Newburgh Arms* came with my thanks from June Knight, who, with Albie, was the last full-time publican, and to Maureen Barry, whose parents were there before. Roland Puttock's family reminiscences, from living at the old alehouse, are gratefully acknowledged too.

My grateful thanks go to His Grace the Duke of Norfolk for permission to access and reproduce information from Arundel Castle archives, and to Sara Rodger, assistant librarian, and her team for their help during my time spent with them.

Thanks also go to Lisa Taylor for permission to reproduce the unique photographs of the site of *The Ship and Lighter*; to Michael Atkin-Berry for details of the sale of *The Victory Inn*; to Bill Beere for recounting his memories of seeing the demolition of *The Red Lion* and his leaning on the bar of so many pubs now long gone; to Arthur Ferrier for his youthful memories of the *General Abercrombie*; and to David Muggleton for information from his articles in *The Quaffer* with the Campaign for Real Ale.

Additional thanks and gratitude go to David Glossop for his family connections with the old pubs, linking his name with the *Bakers Arms*; Eileen Herrington for confirming that the dancing bear in Arundel did feature in the old history of Arundel; Derek Hanson and Chris Goy for help with the history and photographs of *The Red Lion*; David Allcock for a copy of Constable's old Swallow Brewery advertisement; and Neil Warner Hare for expounding his family connections with the *Norfolk Arms* and early transport facilities in Arundel.

For permission to include photographs from other sources I am most grateful to James Cartland (from his *Arundel: A Picture of the Past*), Nicholas Thornton (from his *Arundel Past and Present*), the West Sussex Records Office archives department (for various old pictures), the Group Editor of the *Chichester Observer* newspaper (for items from the *South of England Advertiser* in 1974) and to the Arundel Museum Society for pictures in their repository.

If any other names of supportive residents and those visitors who delighted in reminiscing over old Arundel have been omitted, my sincere apologies and thanks to all of them, for without their contributions parts of this book would have been the poorer.

References to the names of inns or taverns, where the definite article was part of its name, vary considerably depending upon source documents, such as hand-written licence books or old indentures copied from vellum originals. In order to maintain consistency, when the public house is named after a human being by name or title, the author has omitted the definite article, and when the public house is named after an animal, bird or thing the author has included the definite article.

Now I can start recounting the husband and wife teams, often with support from their children, who managed the ale and beerhouses of old Arundel, and of those remaining few that still retail the products of brewing, whose family names are a memorial to the history of the town.

Bibliography

Article

Caldecott, J.B., 'Sussex Taverns in 1636', Sussex Archaeological Society, vol. 79 (1938)

Books

Department of the Environment, Fourth List of Buildings of Special Architectural or Historic Interest as at 7 October 1974, District of Arun (that part comprising the former Borough of Arundel)

Eustace, G.W., *Arundel: Borough and Castle* (1922)

Walkerley, Rodney L., *Sussex Pubs* (1966)

Wright, C., *Arundel Castle* (1818)

Copyright holders

James Cartland and Nicholas Thornton for permission to use pictures from their books on Arundel

WSRO list the pictures via Chief Archivist

The *South of England Advertiser* via Colin Channon at the Chichester Observer Newspapers

Arundel Museum Society for all the pictures in the repository of the Arundel Museum

Chris Goy for permission to include old pictures of the *Red Lion*

I

ARUNDEL ON THE RIVER ARUN

> I feel no pain dear mother now,
> But oh, I am so dry!
> O, take me to a brewery,
> And leave me there to die.
> Parody of *The Collier's Dying Child* by Edward Farmer 1809-76

Arundel is strategically placed in one of the six Rapes, established by the Normans, which divide the County of Sussex more or less equally. Each extends northwards from the English Channel with its own stretch of coastline, a castle for administration and defence, a forest and a river and lies between the Isle of Wight and the chalk ridge of the South Downs. According to folklore etymology, the name has its origin in the French *hirondelle* (swallow). Support for this explanation lies in the fact that a swallow-like bird, with chestnut-red throat, cranked wings and well-forked tail (though without tail-streamers), is depicted in the town's coat of arms. The fact that the word 'martlet', a heraldic footless bird, describes the coat of arms image more accurately, and so refutes the *hirondelle* theory.

However, the historic source of its name, recorded in Domesday Book as *Harundel*, stems from the Old English *hārhūne dell* (horehound valley). White or Common Horehound (*Marrubium vulgare*) is a plant native to Europe belonging to the Lamiaceae family, resembling mint in appearance, and would have grown in abundance in dry wasteland on uncultivated areas. Extracts from such a plant have been used from ancient times as remedies for coughs, croups, colds, the healing of wounds and as an anthelmintic for destroying and expelling intestinal worm infections. Ointments made from natural medicinal herbs long preceded the National Health Service as service to the medieval household.

One American visitor in 1975 even pronounced his overt knowledge of English history by suggesting a variation of the Domesday explanation as coming from the word 'Arunda', a reedy plant growing near rivers. His botanical knowledge had not taken into account that *Arundo donax* was not native to Britain and is so invasive as to out-compete indigenous species and destroy riparian ecosystems, which is what had transpired in California when it was introduced in the early 19th century to assist erosion control in drainage canals. Being one of the fastest-growing terrestrial plants in the world in its native Middle East, it is hardly likely to have been found in the Arun Valley without being noticed. The earlier name for Arun was *Tarrant*, relating to the Roman name *Trisantona*. This was based on the Celtic root word *sent*, which meant 'wanderer' (a meandering river) or 'flooding', which in the latter sense certainly applies to the Arun, particularly during spring tides, and around Amberley, north of Arundel. However, it was the Saxons who dominated once the Romans had gone and they would have been content with the name 'Arun' for the river and, since their name for valley was 'dell', the valley of the Arun would be 'Arundell', recorded as such in many subsequent documents.

With the mudflats of Selsey Bill, the rocks near Bognor and the shifting sandbanks off Pevensey, coastal trade was kept to a minimum but it gave Arundel an advantage thanks to its broad tidal river, and with it a long history as a port and shipbuilding centre. Horse-drawn road transport of raw materials such as coal, timber, salt and building materials comprising stone and chalk for lime-making was difficult due to the inadequacy of the roads with their steep hills and poor surfaces. With a navigable river from the coast in the south to beyond Pulborough in the north, together with connecting canals, transport of such bulky and heavy materials was undertaken by sea-going coastal ships of up to 300 tons and barges, either sailing up or being towed upstream as far as the road bridge or poled beyond, until towpaths were built for horse-drawn traffic. From the mid-16th century the River Arun was navigable without locks for 13½ miles from Little Hampton to Houghton and 11½ miles from Houghton to Pallingham.

In addition, fishing boats brought local catches upstream and sold them at the fish quay near the town bridge. Shipyards and quays on the north bank and sizeable docks and quays on the south bank were the principal source of the growth of the town until the mid-19th century, when the end of the conflict with Napoleonic Europe reduced the need for military and naval activities for coastal defence and warship building.

The farsightedness of landowners of the time, particularly George Wyndham, 3rd Earl of Egremont, in investing in the development of the Rother Navigation and Arun Navigation companies and linking the dockyards at Portsmouth with traffic north, brought wealth and prosperity to Arundel and other townships. The abundance of manual labour enabled the tortuous loops of the Arun around Pulborough to be shortened by the construction of the Coldwaltham Cut and the tunnel under Hardham Hill, a magnificent feat of engineering for the day. Commercial traffic ceased in 1930, brought about by the spread of railways across West Sussex in competition with the waterways and improvements in road transport. The final death knell for the passage of masted ships was the electrification of the railway and the replacement of the retractable bridge over the river, used by steam locomotion, by a fixed bridge.

To satisfy the thirst of itinerant sailors, labouring shipwrights, sawmill operators and attendant trades, the town had been blessed with ale and beerhouses and its own maltsters and brewers. Ale and beer were safer to drink than water, since during the brewing process the product was boiled for one and a half hours. Rural areas such as Sussex did not receive piped water until the late 19th century, and some parts of Arundel not until the mid-20th century, which helped to maintain the sale of ales and beers.

Two words in our language synonymous with brewing are 'ale' and 'beer'. The origin of the word *ale* comes from the Old English *alu* and the Old Norse *ol*, whereas the word *beer* comes from the Old English *bēor*, equivalent to Middle Low German, the Middle Dutch *Bēr*, and the Old High German *Bior* (Dutch, German *Bier*). Only English retains both *ale* and *beer* to describe the products of malting barley. The words used to describe premises selling the products of brewing vary, depending on the facilities they offer. The word 'inn' comes from the Old English and Old Norse *inni,* implying a dwelling place, a hostelry, where all creature comforts are available; 'tavern' from the Old French *taverne*, the Latin *taberna*, which stemmed from Roman occupation; and the word 'hotel' from the French *hotel*, where the words describe a public residence for strangers and travellers alike.

Sussex during Roman occupation appears to have had a warmer climate than in later centuries, and the countryside round Arundel was covered with vineyards, from which excellent wine was made, encouraged by the love of wine brought by these early invaders.

1 *1785 map of Arundel (from Door Book of Families).*

II

Early Taverns and the Emergence of Ale and Beerhouses

With the passage of time, wine production led to the creation of taverns for the sale of wine by retail under the control of the Vintners Company of London. Those who imported wine were known as 'vinetarii' and those retailing it 'tabernarii'. This was approved by a charter granted by Elizabeth I in 1567 specifically naming tavern-keepers outside London and endorsed the earlier Act of Parliament decreed by Edward VI, which sought to impose price-fixing and control excess back-lane wine production, particularly in London. Ten years later this restriction was lifted and, in 1612, by the authority of James I, rights were granted to enable taverns to be set up in any port and town on the common highway, even though restrictions on numbers were still imposed. This enabled two taverns in Arundel to be licensed to Michael Henning and Elizabeth Freeman. Outside London tavern names were rarely applied to hostelries. They were more usually denoted by hanging bushes outside, showing that wine was retailed on the premises.

However, earlier records indicate that there were three inns in the late 16th century – the *George* (1570), *The White Horse* (1571) and the *Crown* (1592), followed in 1625 by the *Kings Arms*. During the Civil War, Parliamentary forces occupied many of the properties in the town during their siege of the castle, utilising the stabling facilities of the inns in the High Street and using many lower rooms of shops and houses for their mounted troops. This accounts for the strange tales passed on by word of mouth relating to the history of this period. One resident, on moving into first-floor apartments, became aware of the smell of beer and the sound of a hurdy-gurdy playing, but after six months both had gone completely!

The map of 1785 taken from the earlier Door Book of Families shows the following named ale/beerhouses on the south side of the River Arun: *The White Horse* (licensed to William Henty) and *The White Hart* (Benjamin Fugar and Thomas Wakeford) in Bridge Street (as it was then) on the right, with *The Dolphin* (James Champion and George Picknell) on the left, before the bridge over the river, which later became the site of *The Bridge Hotel* as a Georgian coaching inn with stabling behind. Over the bridge the map shows *The Swan* (William Lucas) and the *Crown* (Ignas Powell) in the Square with an archway for coaches leading to the yard behind with stabling; a large building halfway up the High Street on the right with access behind for coaches and stabling, which was the *Norfolk Arms* (built between 1782 and 1785 by the Duke of Norfolk); and the *George* (George Blanch) in the High Street with access behind for coaches leading to stabling. The High Street continues into the road to London to the west of St Nicholas' Church via Mary Gate and the site of *The Bell* (William Pierson), which is now gone. It was replaced much later by *The St Mary's Gate* on the corner of Pannets Pond Lane, now called King Street, near the site of the house occupied by the Rev. William and Mrs Groome. William Groome LLB was Vicar of Arundel from 1780 to 1811.

From this corner the lane leads down to Old Market Street (now Maltravers Street), housing the wealthier merchants and property owners, where, on the corner with a lane previously known as Poorhouse Hill and now called Park Place, is the site of *The Ship* (Charles Bushby). Halfway along is the steep lane down to the *Kings Arms* on the corner with Tarrant Street. Then, further along Old Market Street towards the High Street before the corner with Short Lane, is the site of *The Sundial*. No other alehouses are specifically identified by name, though there were many unlicensed houses selling ale during the 16th and 17th centuries as river-borne traffic and trading increased. A building in the lane leading down from Tarrant Street to the river suggested that it could have been a beerhouse or even a brothel, not far from where *The Jolly Sailors* was, now identified as Sailor's Cottage in River Road.

Early records show that there were some twenty premises selling ales or beers, with the distinction in 1824 between the granting of licences to alehouse keepers (allowed to sell ale for consumption on and off the premises) and beerhouse keepers (licensed to sell beer for consumption on the premises only). However, research into a variety of sources, even those unsubstantiated by other corroborative evidence and simply from hearsay or folklore, has revealed a total of 40 establishments dispensing the products of brewing. Some of these names are just relics of a long-lost past, found only in ancient documents, or in articles by writers of the time with their origins unidentifiable. The complete list is recorded by the author's remit to ensure that nothing is lost to posterity, dividing it into those registered as alehouses or beerhouses and those pre-dating the 18th-century licensing requirements.

The distinction between the two words 'ale' and 'beer' has been brought about by the legislation governing the issuing of licences and does reflect the differences in malting or brewing techniques to produce darker or stronger products such as stout and porter. It can reflect, however, a country of origin of the products of brewing. The UK is unique in that establishments are retailing both ale and beer, whereas in such countries as Germany or Holland there is only beer or '*bier*' on sale, while in those of Scandinavia only ale is sold. In 1903 advertisements by brewers, such examples are India Pale Ale from the Swallow

Brewery and a range of ales and beers of different properties from the Lambert & Norris Eagle Brewery. A 1960 beer mat relic from Berlin advertises beer only as Berliner Bier.

Many of the retailing premises were located along the town-side bank of the river among the wharves, shipyards and coal yards catering for the crews unloading ships and barges. Ancillary trades, comprising wheelwrights, blacksmiths, coal-heavers and sawyers, all employed manual workers who would turn to the nearby beerhouses along the river lanes, up into Tarrant Street and then over the bridge into Queen Street. Workers coming into Arundel from Ford would frequent those in Surrey Street and School Lane at the west end of Tarrant Street. In addition to shipping traffic, road traffic bringing passengers into the town by stagecoach from London and Brighton expected the inns and hotels to provide stabling and coach houses, such services being provided by hostelries in Queen Street and High Street. Inns along Maltravers Street and London Road catered for the more affluent residents in the larger houses away from the river and nearer the castle.

Research into indentures held in the castle archives shows that the upper end of the High Street was known as High Market Street and the London Road swept round north of the 14th-century St Nicholas' Church and through Mary Gate (now within the castle grounds). In 1794 *The Bell* was also called *The Blue Bell* (Samuel Woolgar). One indenture named a grocer, Thomas Drewett, abutted to the north-east by 'The Castlehanger' (a name not immediately identified as an inn), and next door *The Star Inn*, occupied by John Hestor. This is corroborated by an indenture dated 1676, held by a private collector, that refers to property in High Market Street in the 'Borough of Arundell' belonging to Thomas Drewett, to the north-west of which was the 'Common Inne' called '*The Starr*' and to the north-east the castle ditch (now filled in but identifiable). Trade tokens of 1657, 1666 and 1667 show Thomas Drewett as a tallow chandler. A later indenture dated 1797 refers to a messuage belonging to John Thorncombe, to the north-west of which was formerly *The Star Inn* and to the north-east the castle ditch, which bears out why it is not marked on the 1785 town plan. Other records around 1756, which have no independent corroboration, relate to a messuage called *The White Horse*, lately known as *The Swan*, in High Market Street, abutting north-east to the castle ditch onto an inn called *The Star*, and fronting to the south-west on to a messuage formerly called *The Spread Eagle*. Reference was also made to *The Swan*, in the lane to the watermill, closing in 1698.

Records in the castle archives relating to the sale in 1714 of messuage or tenements, a slaughterhouse and gardens in High Market Street, sometimes called *The Three Mariners*, refer to the east part in Minsing Lane and then to the west part as bearing the sign *The Red Lion and Anchor*. This property was owned by William and John Hayward and his wife Mary. In the same indentures, reference is made in 1758 to the Rev. Thomas Lear and John Gilbert and, later, in 1793, to Elizabeth Gilbert (spinster and heir to John Gilbert). These are links with the future ownership of these properties. The fact that the 1785 plan of Arundel shows the name John Gilbert alongside the site of *The Red Lion*, and that of Elizabeth Gilbert in Bridge Street, does lend credence to the assumption that the sign of *The Red Lion and Anchor* refers to the inn of similar name adjacent to the *Crown Inn*, and that the passageway between was in fact Minsing Lane, which does extend across Crown Yard to exit alongside the site of the old beerhouse *The Heart in Hand* in Tarrant Street. Another indenture relates to a messuage in High Market Street (which was renamed High Street in 1763) dated 1756, and again refers to John Gilbert and the slaughterhouse that was sometimes known under the sign of *The Three Mariners*. It also mentions the property on the east of Mincing Lane and on the west at the sign of *The Red Lion and Anchor*. The indenture later refers in 1766 to the freehold High Street messuage that James Burt owned as being near the Butchers Shambles. This relates to that part of Old Market Street and its junction with High Street. Another of the castle archive indentures that mentions 'Minsinge Lane' relates to the High Market Street sign of *The Three Mariners* on a messuage formerly called *The Red Lion and Anchor* that by 1793 had dropped the 'and Anchor' and become *The Red Lion*. Differences in spelling reflect the disparity between such documents. All are handwritten on vellum by many different people over long periods and are not generally originals. What is significant, however, is that the names of these old inns and taverns are preserved by their being given to other such hostelries in different parts of Arundel.

Providing the ales and beers, going back to the early 18th century, were a number of brewers, the most notable being the breweries operated by the Constable and Puttock families. Thomas Constable, then living in Old Market Street, was married to the sister of George Puttock, also living in Old Market Street, as shown on the 1785 map of Arundel. The earliest-known brewery at this time was 'The Old Brewery', off Tarrant Street down Brewhouse Hill, as it was known in the early 18th century. Records show this brewery as being sold in 1733 by Philip Newman to Henry Caplin and then, after a series of sales between local property owners, ending up with Edward Puttock in 1780. Puttock was recorded in the 1785 Land Tax and the Universal British Directory of Trades of 1793-8 as a common brewer. He then proceeded to buy various parts of the brewery site piecemeal until, with complicated multiple-ownerships, the 'Eagle Brewery' emerged in the early 19th century. He remained in partnership with Robert Watkins, then steward to the Duke of Norfolk.

It should be noted that Stephen Wise had bought the Old Brewhouse in 1810 and then sold it in 1829 to Robert Watkins. The brewery was bought in 1839 by William Osborne (brewer) and William Duke (gentleman), who ran it as a partnership until 1872, when it was sold, with six public houses, to Henry Harrison. Harrison, after building up the business to include 23 public houses, sold the business in 1879. The final people to brew on site were Isaac Lambert and Edward Norris, who in 1897 formed a limited company and traded as Lambert & Norris Ltd, brewers and maltsters, and then became the

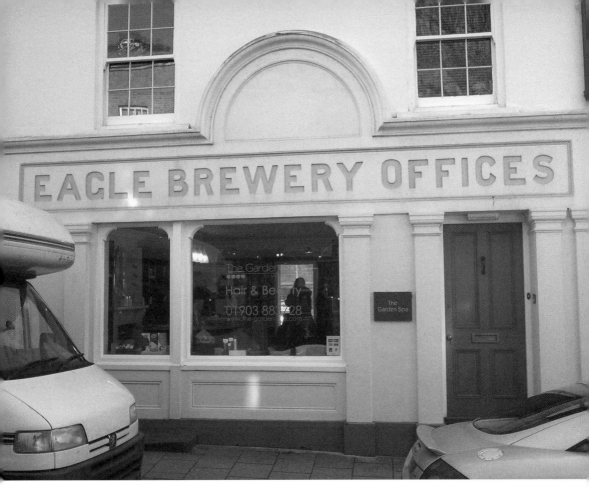

2 *Eagle Brewery Offices.*

Eagle Brewery. The remains of their offices, now a private house, can still be seen in Tarrant Street. In 1910 the company was sold to Friary's of Guildford. From that date it would appear that brewing ceased and the premises simply became agents for Friary's products until trading ceased in 1935.

The adoption of the word 'Eagle' is as shrouded in obscurity as the name 'The Arundel Brewery', since *The Eagle* public house (so named) was not recorded as a licensed house until 1889, and no reference to the name has been found prior to that. However, it seems likely that with the purchase of the Old Brewhouse, Robert Watkins could have been responsible for the change of name, particularly since the castle archives hold an original record of a sale by auction conducted by the Arundel Brewery, held in 1829 and covering a ten-mile radius of premises in Arundel and 'Little Hampton'.

In 1798 George Puttock had built a malthouse and oasthouse on the east side of Bridge Street, commemorated by the engraving on the wall that bears his initials, 'GP 1798'. These supplemented and later replaced the original malthouse on Brewhouse Hill, still remembered as a name on the private residences The Old Malthouse and Malthouse Cottage, below *The Eagle* in Brewery Hill.

A malthouse was started by George Constable in South Marsh (the name being retained by the present-day Malthouse Close), with a brewery on the

3 *Oast house.*

west side of Bridge Street that became known as the Swallow Brewery, now long gone. Its site first became a cinema, then a petrol station and is now a development for retirement homes.

Two significant political events influencing the numbers and survival prospects of the inns and taverns of the time were the Cromwell's domination following the Civil War of the mid-17th century and the rise of French militarism in Europe following the French Revolution, lasting from the end of the 18th century until the defeat of Napoleon in 1815 at Waterloo.

4 *G.S. Constable and Sons' Swallow Brewery.*

The first event was the 18-year war started in 1642 by the raising of the Royalist flag under Charles I against the Puritan Parliamentarians under Oliver Cromwell. The effect on Arundel was brought about by its occupation, initially by the King's forces and then by the forces of Cromwell. The Parliamentarian force was of considerable strength and was commanded by William Waller. The town stayed occupied until the restoration of the monarchy in 1660. The siege of the castle caused considerable devastation to the town itself, as described in a letter written by the wife of the castle governor appointed by the Parliamentarians: 'When we came to Arundel we were met with a most dismal sight, the town being depopulated, and all windows broken with the great guns and the soldiers making stables in the shops and the lower rooms.'

Arundel had become a garrison town and during that time the town wall was demolished, together with the west wing of the castle to make it uninhabitable. Although it was plain that the Parliamentarians were at least as responsible for damaging the town as the Royalists, after the war Arundel Corporation, of which most were Parliamentarians themselves, signed the petition for claiming damages and placed the blame squarely on to the Royalists:

> The sad and distressed state of the poor, plundered, robbed and spoiled inhabitants of the said Borough, who were driven by the King's forces from their house and habitation to secure our lives, and in our absence robbed and spoiled of all outwards comforts to maintain a livelihood, some of our houses to be pulled down, and all our goods embezzled and taken away to our great impoverishment.

The petition was successful in obtaining the large sum of £3,772 7s. 6d. for 36 named inhabitants.

The second event, at the beginning of the 19th century, required an enormous build-up of military and naval strength in southern England to stand up against Napoleon. The consequential demand on accommodation and provision of victuals caused such 'distress' to innkeepers and publicans residing within the Upper Division of Arundel Rape that they humbly petitioned the Hon. Secretary of War:

> It sheweth that the burthen of supporting His Majesty's Forces, marching through this Division, is becoming intolerable, and must, unless some speed of relief be given to your Petitioners, prove their utter ruin, that within the last 4 months, 7,000 troops have been quartered on your Petitioners, in providing them with victuals and other necessities. We have lost £375, & £225 within the last 8 days. We are in general poor and unable to bear such loss and the inconvenience of lodging such of His Majesty's Forces to this extent is too great, as to prevent us from further accommodating the travellers and people usually resorting to our houses. We therefore humbly pray that our suffering may be considered and such relief be given as will render us compensation for the loss sustained during the last 8 days and prevent this loss in future.

This was dated Arundel 3 December 1807 and signed by the following:

William Balchin	*Norfolk Arms*	rent £110
John Moorey	*Crown*	rent £51
John Pullen	*The Red Lion*	rent £18
John Brooks	*The Swan*	rent £23
Henry Hammond	*The White Hart*	rent £10
John Hersee	*The Wheatsheaf*	rent £16
Robert Glossop	*The St Mary's Gate*	rent £18
John Elliott	*The White Horse*	rent £10
unocc.	*Newburgh Arms*	rent -
Edward Stallard	*The Dolphin*	rent £30
Edward Bishopp	*Kings Arms*	rent £18
Edward Elliott	*The Old Ship*	rent £12

It is apparent that very little relief was afforded, for the following memorandum was written by Robert Browning, Quartermaster General:

> Arundel has been of late unavoidably much exposed to the inconvenience of quartering troops upon the march, notwithstanding every endeavour on the part of this office to lessen the burden. The circumstances of remuneration rest with the Secretary of War, but cannot be recommended, as it would be opening a door for numberless similar applications.
>
> Horse Guards 9th December 1807.

III

SOURCES OF EVIDENCE

Some reference documents and sources of information are recorded below to give the reader guidance concerning the breakdown of details as applied to alehouses and beerhouses under their respective names. There are inconsistencies between records because of disparity of sources and the author's reluctance to interpret and amend to create a non-proven uniformity.

WEST SUSSEX LAND TAX, 1785

List of property and house owners as named on the 1785 Arundel street map:

Charles Bushby: owned the storehouse near *The Ship* (at the end of Old Market Street near corner with Poorhouse Hill now Park Place) and the fourth house up from Tarrant Street on the High Street.

John Shaft: owned the large house in Old Market Street opposite *The Sundial* near the corner with Short Lane (see also Thomas Shaft, High Street end-but-one from corner with Old Market Street) and the storehouse in Ship Yard.

George Picknell: owned the house next to *The Dolphin* in Bridge Street (now Queen Street) and the brewhouse and malthouse.

Richard Coote/Thomas Coote: owned the Old Brewhouse in Old Market Street (forerunner of Eagle Brewery) behind the site of *The Eagle*, almost adjacent to the nursery and garden owned by James Newman. The Old Brewhouse was sold in 1780 to Thomas Goble, from whose widow Edward Puttock bought a strip of land to the east and north in 1782.

John Ibbetson: owned two adjoining houses in Farmers Lane (now Parsons Hill) and a malthouse.

Edward Puttock: owned a large house in Old Market Street, midway between Short Lane and what is now Kings Arms Hill. The house is likely to be site of 31 Maltravers Street (*The Wheatsheaf Inn*). He also owned an old brewhouse and malthouse over the bridge (later Swallow Brewery) and bought a strip of land and a building known as 'Green Stall' on the south side of the brewery.

Edward Putton: the tenant in Richard Hersee's house on the corner of Short Lane and Tarrant Street.

Henry Weller: owned a large house on the left-hand side of Tarrant Street and a malthouse.

THE DIRECTORY OF PIGOT & CO.

In 1793-8 it showed:

Public houses:
  Norfolk Arms – George Blanch
  Crown Inn – John Pell

Victuallers:
  James Champion – *The Dolphin*
  Edward Elliott – *The Old Ship*
  Thomas Farrell – no premises identified
  William Lucas – *The Swan*
  John Macklin – *The Sundial*
  John Pullen – *The Red Lion*
  Edward Puttock as a common brewer
  Thomas Smith – *The Jolly Sailors*

In 1839 it showed:

Maltsters:
  George Constable in Queen Street
  Charles New in Tarrant Street
  Osborne and Duke in Tarrant Street

Public houses as:
  The Red Lion – Mary Morley
  The White Hart – Richard Parish
  The Wheatsheaf – unoccupied
  The St Mary's Gate – John Hunt
  General Abercrombie – John Boxall
  Newburgh Arms – Thomas Cousins
  The Old Ship – John Searle

and added
  Kings Arms - Caroline Hersee
  The Black Rabbit – James Oliver

but omitted (as being regarded as hotels):
  The Swan – John Pannett
  The Bridge Hotel – George Young

Sources of Evidence

THE ARUNDEL BREWERY SALE BY AUCTION, 1829

For items in Arundel the list included the following:

Wise's Brewery, below Tarrant Street with access to the river. William Balchin named as tenant.

Wise's Malthouse in Old Brewhouse Yard. George Newman named as tenant.

The Old Brewhouse Estate with blacksmiths and malthouse.

Included in the auction list as inns then owned by the Arundel Brewery were:

The Swan Inn, with Stephen Challen as tenant at will.

Kings Arms, facing Ann Street (an early name for Arun Street or a typographical error or misreading of handwritten copy for type-setting) with William Street.

The Wheatsheaf, with John Hersee as licensed victualler.

Abercrombie public house with George Street.

The White Hart public house with James Stallard and a Mr Allen as occupant.

The Black Rabbit with James Poltick.

Details contained in the auction manifesto have been incorporated within the sections covering these named alehouses.

THE 1824 REGISTER OF LICENSED PREMISES is a definitive source of information confirming the existence of most of those establishments that have a recognisable name, together with that of the publican.
Registered as alehouse keepers:

Norfolk Arms – Thomas Newman
Crown Inn – Richard Ade
The Red Lion – Richard Pannett (could have been Parrish)
The Swan – John Pannett
The White Hart – James Stallard
The Wheatsheaf – John Hersee
The St Mary's Gate – Elizabeth Glossop
General Abercrombie – George Street
Newburgh Arms – William Stone
Kings Arms – William Street
The Bridge Hotel – George Young
The Old Ship – Edward Elliott

Registration continued without much change until John Hersee died in 1829 and *The Wheatsheaf* remained unoccupied, pending a new licensee being found. Edmund Forrest, licensee of the *The Bridge Inn*, died in 1834 and was succeeded by his widow Rhoda Forrest, to whom the licence was given in 1835. Similarly, when William Morley, a new licensee of *The Red Lion*, died in 1835, his widow Mary was made the licensee the following year. It appeared that Caroline Hersee waited a while before taking over the licence of the *Kings Arms* in 1836, which she must have managed for some time. In 1862 it was recorded that she was the licensee of the *Bakers Arms*. In 1838 John Searle took over the licence for *The Old Ship* but appears to have lived only a short while longer, as he was followed by his widow Elizabeth as licensee in 1840. By 1847 it was licensed to Edward Overington, who managed the premises until his death in 1859, when it was taken over by his widow Elizabeth.

From 1893-7 came the names of those registered as beerhouse keepers:
In 1893:

Bakers Arms – William Monk, supplied by Constable

From 1893-7:

The Ship and Lighter – John William Slaughter, supplied by Constable
The Jolly Sailors – Richard Hulls, supplied by Lambert & Norris
The Victory Inn – William Sharp, supplied by Lambert & Norris
The Hare and Hounds – James Slaughter, supplied by Constable
Queens Arms – Thomas Wakeford, supplied by Constable
Bakers Arms – William Jupp Slaughter, supplied by Constable
The White Horse – Frank Slaughter, supplied by Constable
The Heart in Hand – William Sermon, supplied by Lambert & Norris. By 1900 the publican at *The Heart in Hand* was Alfred Hulls.

THE POST OFFICE DIRECTORY OF 1862 confirms much of the same information about the names of people managing licensed premises on a street-by-street basis, but frequently does not identify the premises by popular name or inn sign. Instead, they are identified by the resident being a 'beer retailer' or 'cooper' (barrel maker), which can, in default, be related to the name of the licensed premises. Those listed by inn sign appear to be the older, more established places, and are recognisable as those licensed to sell on-and-off the premises, such as *The White Hart, Kings Arms, Crown, General Abercrombie* and the like.

High Street	William Baker – *The Swan*
	Henry Randall – *The Red Lion*
	William Watts – *Crown*
King Street	Charles Bone – soda water and ginger beer
	John Burchell – beer retailer – premises not identified
	Elizabeth Overington – *The Old Ship*
London Road	George Hersee – *The St Mary's Gate*
Queen Street	Stephen Kinchitt – *The White Hart*

	James Parish – *The Bridge Inn*
	John Richards – cooper – *General Abercrombie*
Maltravers Street	James Daughtrey – beer retailer – *Bakers Arms*
	Fred Lucas – *The Wheatsheaf*
Mount Pleasant	John Lancaster – beer retailer – *The Chestnut*
Surrey Street	Sarah Roe – beer retailer – *The Hare and Hounds*
Ship Yard	William Smith – beer retailer – *The Jolly Sailors*
	George Upfold – beer retailer – premises not identified
Tarrant Street	Willliam Lewis Burrell – *Newburgh Arms*
	John Burton – beer retailer and cooper – *Brewers Arms*
	William Corbett – *Kings Arms*
	Charles Ford – beer retailer – premises not identified
	Caroline Hersee – beer retailer – *Kings Arms*
	Osborne and Duke – brewers and maltsters
	Edward Peckham – cooper working with John Burton
	William Wakeford – beer retailer – *Queens Arms*
	Edward Witham – beer retailer – *The Red Lion*

Although the names of John Lancaster and James Daughtrey appear in census returns 1851 and 1861 as beer retailer and beerhouse keepers there is no direct correlation with beerhouse premises and names in the census. Licence records have shown that James Daughtrey was at the *Bakers Arms* and, though *The Chestnut* in Mount Pleasant (Poor House Lane) has been associated with John Lancaster and wife Sarah, there is no documentary corroboration. However, a late resident of King Street, who had taken up residence in 1956, had met an Irishman who had acted as a gang leader recruiting itinerant labourers for the restoration works being carried out at the castle during the late 19th century. In addition, he used to collect jugs of beer from a beerhouse on the corner of Bond Street and Mount Pleasant to supply the needs of the men working on the castle rebuild. Such evidence gives credence to establishing the location of a beerhouse in Mount Pleasant that was attributed to John Lancaster and bore the name *The Chestnut*. Its existence has been perpetuated by word-of-mouth over the years, together with that of *The Yew Tree*.

Likewise, Fanny Seagrave's name has been linked with *The Mount Pleasant* in Tarrant Street, with no evidence yet found to confirm this or the location of a beerhouse with this name. However, previous generations now deceased have assured the writer by word-of-mouth that it existed opposite the *Kings Arms*. This hearsay was included in writings by an early curator of the Arundel Museum and Heritage Centre, and printed in the *West Sussex Gazette* in October 1974 with even vaguer references to the *Carpenters Arms* in Mill Lane. According to other hearsay sources, this was reputedly opened in 1841 but closed before 1850, as was the *Bricklayers Arms*, also in Mill Lane.

PIKE'S BLUE BOOK OF 1910-11 provides authentic evidence of the licensee linked with the licensed premises at the time.

>William Sharp – *The Victory*
>J.E. Elwood – *The Red Lion*
>E.A. Hare (Mrs) – *Norfolk Arms*
>W.E. Glossop – *The Old Ship*
>E.A.G. Hersee – *The St Mary's Gate*
>H.W. Calcutt – *The Wheatsheaf Inn*
>M.A. Hulls (Mrs) – *The Heart in Hand*
>C.S. Arbery – *The Eagle Inn*
>Thomas Wakeford – *Queens Arms Inn*
>J.H. Roger – *Kings Arms Inn*
>M.F. Booker – *Newburgh Arms Inn*
>E.G. Hulls – *The Jolly Sailors*
>E. Slaughter – *General Abercrombie*
>F. Stevens – *The White Hart*
>A.G. Parsons – *The White Horse Inn*
>Miss Challen – *The Bridge Hotel*
>Mrs Mary J. Stevens – *The Swan*
>E.C. Peake – *The Railway Hotel*
>Mary J. Stevens (Mrs) – *The Swan Hotel*
>Miss Challen – *The Bridge Hotel*

Managing these alehouses and beerhouses appeared to be too stressful for the men. Records contained in the Licensing Minute Book of 1916 to 1920 show that widows were licensees for the *Norfolk Arms* (Elizabeth Ann Hare), *The Swan* (Mary Jane Stevens followed by Alice Boswell), *General Abercrombie* (Ellen Slaughter), *Newburgh Arms* (Frances Booker), *The Mile House/The White Swan* (Fanny Jupp) and, for beerhouses, the *Queens Arms* (Eliza Wakeford) and *The Heart in Hand* (Mary Ann Hulls).

Following the French Revolution and the political upheaval in Europe, together with the dominance of Napoleonic France, military activity increased and Arundel became a significant holding area for the build-up of British forces leaving for the continent to fight with Prussia against Napoleon. The *Norfolk Arms* was occupied by troops awaiting embarkation to the Continent for many years during this period. Many of the French prisoners of war arriving in Britain were absorbed into the environs of Arundel, where they could have contributed to building houses in the town itself.

Naval victories under Nelson and the dominance of the river traffic influenced the naming of some of the beerhouses trading around the shipyards of the Arun itself, such as *The Victory* in Bond Street, *The Ship* in Maltravers Street, which moved in time to *The Old Ship* in King Street (where many of the houses, it is reputed, were built by French prisoners-of-war), *The Jolly*

Sailors and *The Ship and Lighter* in Ship Yard itself. It is likely that *The Old Ship* was trading as such in 1805, though there is no sign of a building on the maps just prior to that period.

The next significant date is 1822 when the Arundel Borough Archives map shows King Street with no houses (which may not be significant as the map is not very clear), though the 1824 Register of Licences shows that *The Old Ship* was owned by Messrs Puttock and Constable, and Pigot's *Directory of Sussex 1828* also refers to *The Old Ship* in King Street among its list of other taverns and public houses. However, there was no reference to *The Victory* until Pike's Blue Book in 1911, even though houses numbered 1 and 3 Bond Street were identified in the 'Fourth List of Buildings of Special Architectural or Historic Interest', compiled by the Department of the Environment and dated October 1974, as having been built in the early 19th century, which suggests that it was built at the same time as *The Old Ship*. Other records show that it had been built by 1829 and was later let by Henry, Duke of Norfolk, to Lambert & Norris Brewery in 1906 and then, with their liquidation, to Friary Brewery in 1935, until it closed down in 1974.

The Old Ship continued as a public house, with ownership moving from the Duke of Norfolk and Henty & Constable to the Brighton brewers Tamplins in 1954, with the licensed premises sold to Friary Holroyd and Healys Brewery of Guildford, until it closed down in 1979-80 with John Farr as its last landlord. It then became a private house and was converted into two separate dwellings.

The Jolly Sailors in River Road was recorded in Pike's Blue Book of 1910-11. The landlord at the time was E.G. Hulls, who was referred to in later records as a beer retailer in Ship Yard. It was closed in 1933-4, when the Hulls family took over *The Heart in Hand* in Tarrant Street, which was owned by the Lambert & Norris Brewery with a first record in Kelly's Directory in 1927.

The challenge is not only to know the location of these extinct alehouse and beerhouse dinosaurs but also to establish what they were like when they were a living part of the community of providers of ale and beer. In fact, the 'Rules of this Tavern', found in researching old records, give a picture of their usage in earlier times:

> 4 pence a night for bed
> 6 pence with potluck
> 2 pence for horse keeping
> No more than five to sleep in one bed
> No boots to be worn in bed
> No razor grinders or tinkers taken in
> No dogs allowed in the kitchen
> Organ grinders to sleep in the wash house

Although this book was intended to record for posterity the memories of those ale and beerhouses that have faded into history, mention must be made of those that have survived to continue serving the produce of the remaining breweries before they too cease to function and are replaced with coffee shops and snack bars, consign those smokers who wish to enjoy the pints they have always enjoyed to the ashtrays lodged on the streetwise window sills. Of those on the list that started back in the 16th century and were shown within the old town wall on the 1785 map, *The White Hart*, *The Swan Hotel*, the *Norfolk Arms* and the *Kings Arms* are still functioning and are joined by *The Red Lion*, *The Eagle* (at one time the *Brewers Arms*) and *The St Mary's Gate*. Additionally included as giving a service to Arundel residents are *The Arundel Park Hotel* (at one time *The Railway Hotel*), *The Black Rabbit* and *The White Swan Hotel* (at one time *The Mile House*).

IV

BEERHOUSES

The **Bakers Arms**' exact location had been in some doubt due to its imprecise address in early records. However, the conveyance dated February 1945 relating to a property adjacent to the Little House, on the corner of Bakers Arms Hill and Maltravers Street, stated 'that the property should not at any time thereafter be used as a hotel, public house or beershop or for the sale of intoxicating liquor'. The operative word in this document was 'thereafter', implying that prior to 1945 it functioned as a 'beershop'. It is described as early 18th century with grey brick headers, red brick dressings and pitched tile roof and it is shown on the 1785 map but not marked as the *Bakers Arms*. However, the adjacent timber-framed cottage being named 'Bakers Arms Cottage' suggests that its larger neighbour was the *Bakers Arms*.

It is first recorded in the Post Office Directory of 1845, with William Gale as its landlord, and it was confirmed in the 1861 census that William Gale, at the age of 86, was registered as beer seller at the *Bakers Arms* in Tarrant Street. A report in the *West Sussex Gazette* of 3 August 1865 referred to a felon being apprehended in the 'Bakers Arms beerhouse, Arundel', indicating that it was a recognised licensed retailer for consumption of beer on the premises. The Arundel Beerhouse Licence Book registered James Daughtrey as licensee in 1869. The 1871 census recorded James Daughtrey as a beer retailer in Maltravers Street with his wife Jane, but did not identify in which beerhouse. However, the 1881 census gives his year of birth as 1809, and his occupation as beerhouse keeper. Further corroboration comes from the Arundel Licence Book, which records that, with James dying in 1882, George Glossop had taken over the *Bakers Arms* temporarily before handing over to Jane Daughtrey, James's widow, for two years, before she too died and Eliza Monk became her will executor, arranging the transfer of the licence to William Monk in January 1885.

The next census of 1891 showed William Monk, born in 1827, registered as publican with wife Eliza, born 1829. Kelly's Directory of 1890 showed W. Monk as beer retailer in Maltravers Street, corroborated by the Arundel Directory of 1892 showing Mr W. Monk as at the *Bakers Arms*, also in Maltravers Street. He

5 *Site of the* Bakers Arms.

remained there until 1893, when it was transferred to William Jupp Slaughter. In the Licence Register of Beerhouse Keepers 1893-7, William Monk was licensee in 1893, followed by William Jupp Slaughter, the beerhouse being supplied by Constable's Brewery. Arundel Beerhouse Licence Book registered Henry Sturt as taking the licence in January 1900 but dying in April, when his widow Fanny became licensee from 14 May 1900. It was then transferred to Thomas Phillip Glossop in March 1906. An application for renewal of licence was then handed over to the Compensation Authority for consideration. It was refused on the grounds that it was redundant to requirements in the area, but a temporary transfer of the licence was awarded to Humphrey William Calcutt in October 1907, when it ceased trading.

The *Bakers Arms'* location on the steep gradient of Bakers Arms Hill suggested that delivery of beer casks could have been difficult, which may have resulted in its ceasing to ply its trade as a beerhouse, particularly with so many other licensed premises nearby in more accessible Tarrant Street. However, research into adjacent premises that possessed very large cellarage suggested that beer casks could have been loaded from the Maltravers Street hatchways down ramps through this cellar and out through rear doors, advantageously using the steep slope of the hill to gain access to the rear wall of the *Bakers Arms*. The pathway followed behind these properties, one branch continuing as far as the site of George Puttock's house (which could have become *The Wheatsheaf Inn*) and the other exiting lower down into Bakers Arms Hill.

The **Brewers Arms** was first recorded in 1863 in the Arundel Beerhouse Licence Book, with John Burton as licensee. He was born in 1805 and was registered in the 1861 census return as a cooper, employing one man, and then as a beerhouse keeper in the returns of 1881 and 1891. He was listed in the Post Office Directory of 1862 as a beer retailer and cooper, working for the Swallow Brewery, as was Edward Peckham, a cooper in Tarrant Street, who could have been his employee. Research showed that John Burton lived with wife Sarah, three years his junior, in a substantial 16th-century timber-framed cottage with

6   *John Burton's cooperage.*

stone roof in Tarrant Street. It was adjacent to the taller three-storey printer and grocery store served by George Edward Slaughter, his wife Frances, daughter Anne Maria and son Edwin. At the far end of the Burtons' cottage there was a barrel-making workshop with double-door access and a sign above displaying, in capital letters, his name and trade as a cooper.

David Steadman became licensee in June 1876 until 1881 when, on 26 September, it was transferred to Thomas Clements for five years. The last licensee at the *Brewers Arms* was William Miles, from March 1886 until May 1889, when it was renamed *The Eagle*. The licence was issued for an alehouse and transferred to Otto John Henry Behrens in June 1889. The Arundel Directory of 1892 showed Mrs Burton, now a widow, residing in Tarrant Street as John Burton had died during 1891, having handed over the running of the *Brewers Arms* to younger men when he had reached his 70th birthday.

The **Queens Arms**, a mid-18th-century brick building, with an east elevation of modular flint and brick dressing, a hipped tile roof and catslide behind, was located at the corner of the extension to Farmers Lane (now Kings Arms Hill) and Tarrant Street opposite the *Kings Arms*. It had three double-hung casement windows at first-floor level and two attic dormers. The main entrance door, with steps up from the street between a shop bow window on the left and a

7   Queens Arms.

shop bay window on the right, each with tripartite double-hung sash windows with glazing bars, led into a large bar room. Inside to the left, curving brick stairs downwards gave access to a small cellar. To the right of the main entrance were additional steps up to a smaller bar room via a door in the bay window with street access to cellarage. It was shown on the 1785 town plan but not identified as an inn; instead it had the name 'John Smith' alongside, adjacent to a large orchard.

The first record was in the 1851 census when William Wakeford, a bricklayer born in 1808, was registered as living there with Louisa Wakeford, born Louisa Pledge in 1816, his wife since 1838. At the next census ten years later he was shown as bricklayer and beerhouse keeper at the *Queens Arms*. The following census showed him as bricklayer and publican, and he was confirmed as a beer retailer in Tarrant Street in the 1862 GPO Directory. The Arundel Beerhouse Licence Book registered William Wakeford as licensee at the *Queens Arms* in 1869, followed in April 1876 by Louisa's name as licensee after William's death. From this period only his widow's name featured as beerhouse keeper, confirmed in the GPO directory of 1874 and Kelly's of 1882, where she was described as a beer retailer.

The couple were fortunate to have ten children baptised. Among them was son Thomas, born in 1852, initially registered as bricklayer, who by the 1891 census had married Eliza from Farlington, born in 1850, and taken over the running of the inn when his mother died in June 1889. Thomas then became licensee until his death in 1909 when in August the licence was transferred to his widow. The Arundel Directory of 1892 showed Mr Wakeford at the *Queens Arms*, followed by the 1893-7 register of licensees showing Thomas Wakeford and Mrs Wakeford as joint publicans. Pike's Blue Book of 1910-11 recorded Mrs Wakeford only and the licensing minute book of 1916-35 showed Eliza Wakeford at the *Queens Arms Inn*, confirming that her husband Thomas had died at the turn of the century. Eliza Wakeford remained as licensee until her death during the winter of 1915 when Ellen Atkins arranged temporary transfer of the licence to Henry Charles Knight in January 1917. He became the licensee until 1924, when his application for a renewal, describing the premises as a beerhouse being supplied by Henty & Constable, was referred to the Compensation Authorities and refused in March 1924.

After ceasing to trade as an inn it became a shop, after which the premises were converted into two private houses, the right-hand one being extended northwards up the hill with car parking access from Kings Arms Hill. Two blocked windows have since been replaced to make a total of five casement windows at first-floor level and an ancient well retained as a feature in the garden behind.

8   *Site of the* Queens Arms.

The Hare and Hounds started life as a beerhouse in the triangular room on the corner of Surrey Street and the path leading to Peartree Cottage. Kelly's Directory of 1855 shows Mrs Sarah Roe as a beer retailer in Surrey Street. She was the widow of Charles Roe, a beer retailer in Tarrant Street. The Arundel Beerhouse Licence Book registered Sarah Roe as licensee of *The Hare and Hounds* in 1863. It also recorded her death in 1871, with Maria Langley appointed to administer her will by arranging transfer of the licence

9 *Site of* The Hare and Hounds.

to George Gumbell for one year, until transfer was made to James Slaughter in 1873. The Post Office Directory of 1874 records James Slaughter as a beer retailer getting supplies from Constable's Brewery. Although the Arundel Directory of 1892 showed that W. Slaughter was at *The Hare and Hounds Inn* it is likely that this was an error in transcription since the family's research shows James Slaughter (baptised in 1830), was at *The Hare and Hounds* in 1892. This is confirmed by the Register of Licensees 1893-9. He had plied his trade initially as a boatman working with Buller and Slaughter, boat proprietors, at 'The Old Bridge House' on the town side of the river bank, marrying Frances Jupp, from whom was born a son, William Jupp Slaughter, in 1868. William later became licensee at the *Bakers Arms*.

An application for renewal of a licence in 1907 was referred to the Compensation Authority, but was refused on the grounds being of unsuitable accommodation for a beerhouse and uneconomic with respect to other premises nearby. It ceased trading in 1908. Of the many elderly residents consulted, who had lived in Arundel all their lives, one, then only four years old, could remember *The Hare and Hounds*, describing vividly how her grandfather, with whom her family had lived to look after him when her grandmother died, would have called in for a drink at a beerhouse opposite the old Church of England school in Surrey Street, and how her aunt was sent from where they lived in Park Bottom to call him home for Sunday dinner.

The Heart in Hand (sometimes remembered as a corruption of *The Hart in Hand*) was located in Tarrant Street and was described as a small drab beerhouse and a pokey little place, with the right-hand door leading into the public bar and an L-shaped bar on the left. Ahead and up a high step was the back room, with dartboard and piano. The street door on the left, giving access to living quarters above, also led into a small snug served via a hatch from the bar itself. The cellars were accessible from the footpath down the side of the building leading to Crown Yard, and from a floor hatch in the back room.

The Arundel Beerhouse Licence Book records George Redman as licensee in 1869 until 13 July 1874, when Charles Hatcher took over. It was then transferred to Arthur Blackman in July 1877 and then to Spencer Reed until August 1879. Foster Richard Duke became publican for two years until September 1881, when the licence was transferred to Edward Keys, who was licensee until his death in March 1883. The licence was then transferred to William Sermon in May, who soldiered on until his death in 1898. The licence was then transferred temporarily to his widow Caroline for two months before going to her son, James Henry, living with the family as a lodger, who carried on until the licence could be transferred to Alfred Hulls in November 1900. Mr W. Sermon was listed in the 1892 Arundel Directory and in the 1893-7 Register of Licensees, as was Alfred Hulls in 1900.

The licence was issued unconditionally in March 1908 to Alfred's widow Mary Ann, remembered affectionately by many

10   The Heart in Hand.

older residents as Mary Greenfield, who stayed in charge until 1948. Mrs M.A. Hulls was listed in Pike's Blue Book of 1911-12 and in the Licensing Minute Book 1916-35 as Mrs Mary Ann Hulls. She was recorded as being a beer retailer in the 1927 Kelly's Directory and named on the inn sign and on the headboard above the window as being supplied by Lambert & Norris. One resident of Tarrant Street recalls Tom Greenfield and his wife in the early 1930s, living at the time at *The Heart in Hand*, organising char-à-banc parties, with Mrs Greenfield banging on a tray up and down Tarrant Street to announce what was going on in support of Tom's sister at *The Heart in Hand*. The Arundel street directory of 1957-8 listed the premises as *The Heart in Hand Inn* with Harry Burch as the last named landlord until its closure in 1960-2 and conversion into a shop.

The Jolly Sailors was located on the town side of the river in Ship Yard, between the timber wharfs below the sawmill to the east and the coal wharf and the Arundel Co-operative Industrial and Provident Society's wharf to the west. It was sandwiched between a four-storey warehouse and terraced cottages ending at the corner of Arun Street where it met the river. It comprised ground-floor accommodation for bars with two staircases leading to bedrooms above. There was

11 The Jolly Sailors.

no cellar because of the problems from frequent springtide flooding, beer being supplied in casks and bottle-crates loaded from the road. The right-hand door gave way to a long flagstone passage covered with sawdust and liberally provided with spittoons. It led to the kitchen quarters and lavatory facilities off-premises in the yard behind. The centre door (now blocked up) opened into the spit-and-sawdust public bar, with the bar itself along the left-hand wall. The left-hand door led into what could have been the saloon bar (if there was one in this type of neighbourhood).

The narrowness of the road itself was compounded when heavy dray horses and loaded wagons attempted to supply the needs of a beerhouse and compete with the pedestrian needs of residents.

Opposite were terraced cottages, with a row of six leading off at right angles known as The Alley. They had flint walls and slate roofs, and the end cottage was made from brick with a tiled roof. The first house, described as derelict, jutted out towards the brewery building and made River Road, as it became known, rather narrow at that point. Each house had its own garden with wooden fences and gate. Front doors gave way to a living room and fireplace with a wood-burning cooking range alongside and a scullery off. A staircase led to two bedrooms on the first floor and a second flight to a large room above in the attic. There was no water, gas, electricity or separate lavatory provided. For water, residents used a standpipe alongside the wall of the adjacent Eagle Brewery, whose dominating buildings encircled this residential enclave. In addition, the brewery also provided lavatory facilities via a narrow door in the wall of the large corrugated-roofed structure that served as stabling and storage for their delivery wagons, with each household having a key.

Two cottages directly opposite *The Jolly Sailors* had two rooms downstairs, a living room with fireplace and a kitchen behind, with a coal-fired stove for cooking, with a staircase from behind a door in the kitchen leading to two bedrooms. From the back one a second staircase led to a large attic bedroom. At the back was a communal courtyard with lavatories for the River Road cottages. The courtyard backs on to the bottom three cottages in Arun Street, from which there was access to the courtyard itself.

A footpath led off River Road between these two cottages and the backs of The Alley houses to an orchard of large pear trees where the landlord kept hens. A low wall separated the courtyard from the path and on it the landlord used to leave pear fallers for the children. Children of the family at the end house remember throwing pears to the men working opposite, their thanks to the children being the passing down of the odd bottle of beer.

The area had achieved notoriety following a fight in which it was reputed that turnips were used as missiles, from which it took its name 'Turnip Green Square'. The clientele visiting the beerhouse itself were sailors from ships that worked up and down the river, who frequently required overnight accommodation pending the unloading and loading of cargoes, sawmill workers from along Ship Yard and coal-heavers from the nearby quays. It was an area typical of seaports with brothels and bawdy houses, where sanitation and sewage were primitive and resultant diseases such as cholera, typhoid and dysentery abounded.

The first record of *The Jolly Sailors* as a beerhouse was in the 1793 Pigot & Co. directory, showing Thomas Smith as a victualler in Ship Yard. Arundel's Beerhouse Licence Book recorded in 1869 that Richard Hulls, born in 1841, was the licensee until March 1900, when his son Ernest George Hulls then became licensee for 30 years. This was confirmed by the 1871 Census, which identified Richard Hulls as a beer retailer at *The Jolly Sailors* with the next return of 1881 recording him as a beerhouse keeper. With wife Ellen (*née* Smith) and a family of five boys and two girls, the Hulls ran the beerhouses of *The Jolly Sailors* and *The Heart in Hand* until their closures. The register of licensees of 1893 recorded Richard Hulls as being supplied by Lambert & Norris Ltd of the Eagle Brewery. Next, Pike's Blue Book of 1911 showed E.G. Hulls as the landlord, with Kelly's Directory of 1927 showing Ernest George Hulls as a beer retailer in River Road. This evidence is authenticated on the inn sign itself and the beer-bottle crates. Additional evidence comes from oral and written memoirs of an informant who lived at the time in The Alley off River Road, knowing them as Mr and Mrs Hulls, who were also their landlords and owned the adjacent orchard. Ernest's wife Agnes provided evening snacks of bread and cheese and bed and breakfast for bargemen.

The 1892 Arundel Directory placed Mr R. Hulls at *The Jolly Sailors* in Ship Yard. In his earlier years, Richard Hulls, while working on the Arundel railway line, lost the lower part of one leg, which was replaced by a wooden peg leg that he wore until his death. Accidents on the river were frequent, with sailors being knocked into the river by swinging booms during ship manoeuvring or simply falling off barges when they swung with the changing tidal currents. Richard Hulls kept a small boat behind *The Jolly Sailors* and used it to rescue any unfortunates who had fallen into the water. He was presented with a silver watch and tea set and an illuminated certificate in his name dated 31 October 1895 from residents of Arundel, 'His Worship the Mayor, Alderman and Messieurs', in appreciation of services unobtrusively rendered for many

12 *The Hulls family, 1925.*

years in rescuing lives and recovering bodies from the River Arun. One tale that came down through the ages was that on one occasion, in his haste, he leapt into his boat and the wooden leg went through the bottom of the hull. His son Richard William became Mayor of Arundel in 1908.

Richard's younger brother William was registered at the age of twenty-one in the 1891 census return as a brewer's clerk, and eventually became manager of the Eagle Brewery in May 1919. This had become the Friary Brewery, following the acquisition by Lambert and Norris of the Eagle Brewery. Land Registry documents showed William also owned properties in Arun Street in 1926, to which reference is made in notes on *The Orchard* (see chapter VI).

13 *Richard 'Pegleg' Hulls.*

Finally, William John Lee had taken over in November 1930 until the licence was not renewed. After reference to the Compensation Authority in February 1932, the old beerhouse ceased trading on the grounds that the premises were unsuitable and the business not viable. As the last remembered landlord, Jack Lee was also the foreman of tree-fellers at the sawmill sited beyond the Arun River Board House on the corner of Brewery Hill and a hundred yards east along the narrow path known as Ship Yard. Memories of the tree-trunk-laden quayside, with the wooden structure of the sawmill and the old salthouse in the distance, are of 'sawdust and stag-beetles' in Hago's yard (Hall and Golding).

In later years, when *The Jolly Sailors* had ceased to ply its beerhouse trade, it became a refuge for displaced residents arising from an unexploded 500lb bomb dropped into woodland adjacent to the Chichester Road during the Second World War. The premises are now divided into two self-contained cottages. The Alley cottages survived until post-Second World War demolition and redevelopment.

The Ship and Lighter, located alongside the blacksmith's workshop of George Stedman in Ship Yard, now River Road, was first recorded as a beerhouse in the 1793 Pigot & Co. Directory, showing Thomas Smith as licensed victualler in Ship Yard without linking to a named beerhouse. On the 1785 town plan there was a building right-angled to an adjacent one approximating to the position of *The Ship and Lighter* and the adjoining blacksmith. The 1862 Post Office Directory named only William Smith and George Upfold as beer retailers, without connecting them with a named beerhouse. The Arundel Beerhouse Licence Book records the name of Erney Bennett as licensee in 1869, followed in 1870 by William Slaughter, but this changed to John William Slaughter in 1872. This was confirmed in the register of licensees of 1893 with his supplies coming from George Constable's Swallow Brewery to *The Ship and Lighter*. Research conducted by the present Slaughter family corroborated the fact that John William Slaughter, once a fisherman, was the publican of *The Ship and Lighter* in later life.

The Beerhouse Licence Book records that John William Slaughter died in January 1907 and the next licence application was made by William Belram, executor to the will. It was then transferred to Edward James Greenfield in January 1907, with a temporary authority to Ernest Arthur Spencer until March 1908, when the renewal application was referred to the Compensation Authority and refused on the grounds of 'redundancy'. The old beerhouse then ceased trading.

It was described as a small intimate place with a single entrance giving way to a door on the right that led into the public bar with a fireplace ahead and a curved bar on the left. It contained one of the last skittle alleys to be in use in a West Sussex beerhouse. To the left at the entrance was the snug, heated from a fireplace, where those who had had enough could sleep it off. Underfloor cellars

14 *(Above and below) Site of* The Ship and Lighter.

were accessible from the yard behind the rear wall where there were stables. The premises, now divided into two, one part used as a veterinary practice and the other a private residence, is adjacent to a cottage named 'Ship & Lighter Cottage'. Recollections of a resident, born in 1823 in Tarrant Street, revealed how busy Ship Yard was at that time, with large barges unloading at a wharf belonging to the Ship and Lighter Company and barges built and repaired by

Henley and Slater. These lend credence to the location and naming of the old beerhouse. Research by the Slaughter family has shown differing derivations and spellings of their name (such as 'Slatter' and 'Slater') and their links with beerhouses and boatmen.

The Victory was a beerhouse on the corner of Bond Street and King Street. It was built of beach flint cobbles and brick outside, chalk blocks inside beneath wooden panelling, and a slate roof, with the main frontage of 63ft and a return frontage of 14ft. Tenancy records, based on research evidence provided by the West Sussex Records Office and Arundel Castle Archives, indicated that the property was first leased from 29 September 1805 to John Downer. The land was occupied earlier by Joseph Hinde and William Connor, bricklayers and builders, and later by Charles Connor and widow Burchell, there being no reference to an inn with the name *The Victory*. If the premises were a beerhouse at the time, the conjecture that it was so named following Nelson's defeat of the French fleet at Trafalgar, or even renamed from an earlier name *The Blue Boar*, is credible.

The Arundel Beerhouse Licence Book records that in 1869 James Jones was licensee, dying shortly after. His widow Mary took over in November 1873 until 1876, when she was succeeded by William Sharp. Corroborative evidence from Pike's Blue Book of 1886 confirmed that William Sharp was the licensee, followed by the 1891 census registering William Sharp, born in 1844, as publican at *The Victory Inn*. This fact was recorded in the 1892 Arundel Directory, confirming that Mr W. Sharp at *The Victory Inn* was also a carrier. The 1893 register of licensees and Pike's Blue Book, dated 1910-11, included William Sharp by name, who was then followed by J. Phillips, whose full name 'Joseph Phillips' appeared above the door lintel shown in the photograph below of *The Victory Inn*, dated 1910 as indicated by the dress of the two bystanders. It

15 The Victory, *1910*.

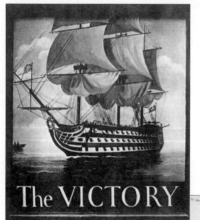

16 The Victory Inn.

shows the hanging sign as *The Victory Inn* with Joseph Phillips being the 'LICENSED RETAILER of BEER to be CONSUMED on the PREMISES'. The later picture shows the wording '*The Victory Inn*' on the front wall, with the hanging sign showing two views of Nelson's flagship HMS *Victory*, as painted by Arundel sign-painter Ralph Ellis (left).

The licence was renewed unconditionally in March 1908 when it was transferred to Joseph Phillips in November 1911 for two years. It was transferred briefly to Richard Blackman in November 1913 until August 1915, when James Collins became licensee for the period of the First World War until October 1919, when it was transferred to James's son, William James Collins, who became the licence holder. However, in 1920 an application for renewal of licence was opposed by the then Police Superintendent, F.J. Peel (a good name for a 'peeler'), who commented that, although there was a public bar, a smoking room and a bottle and jug department, with 14 other fully licensed premises and five beerhouses there was more than enough to cater for Arundel's then population of 2,842. With two other houses nearby, *The Old Ship* round the corner in King Street and *The St Mary's Gate* 150 yards away in London Road, in his opinion these other houses supplied ample accommodation for the neighbourhood.

Mr Cross of the licensing authority, in considering the application, said that *The St Mary's Gate* was as much for the working class as *The Victory*, though it was in fact used mostly for teas. All these houses got their fair share of the working class and, with *The St Mary's Gate* doing the best, he considered that the other two houses met the needs of the immediate neighbourhood. He could not say that this house did the best of all three – it was the smaller of the other two, which were fully licensed, whereas *The Victory* was only a beerhouse, but it was in demand and was well conducted. Police Sgt H.G. Cuff had taken measurements from *The Victory* to *The Old Ship* – 72 yards – and to *The St Mary's Gate* – 128 yards.

The applicant, William Hulls, of Lambert & Norris, owners of one fully licensed house and three beerhouses, said that trade had been improving and, of the three houses, *The Victory* was doing better than the other two, especially as *The St Mary's Gate* catered essentially for visitors to Arundel and tea parties. William James Collins, licensee, had done an attendance check and confirmed for 14 Feb – 35, 19 Feb – 52, 20 Feb (Sunday) – 15, 27 Feb – 14, 3 Mar – 49, and he had obtained 700 signatures supporting the licence application. H.W. Taylor of 16 Bond Street had used the house since 1885 and Richard Northeast, also of Bond Street and a member of a well-known family, had used it for 50 years. The meeting concluded with a unanimous decision to renew the licence.

William Collins continued as licensee until just before the outbreak of the Second World War. In April 1939 his unmarried sister Susan Emily Collins had, with her sixty-year-old brother, taken over briefly before handing over to Ernie Street in 1940. The 1916-35 licensing minute book indicated that in 1920 William J. Collins was the licensee, and he was confirmed in the 1938 Kelly's Directory as publican. A resident living in Bond Street, born in Arundel and attending the Roman Catholic junior school, confirmed from memory that William (James) Collins was still the licensee just prior to the Second World War and that Sergeant Cuff and Superintendent Peel were in charge of the Arundel police station in Maltravers Street.

During the war and after, Ernie Street managed *The Victory*, leaving in 1948 to take over *The Old Ship* in King Street, transferring the licence for a year in November to James Herbert Oxley. In May 1949 Charles Joel became licensee, with Maimie, his widow, taking over *The Victory* until 1953. She was helped by daughter Paula, who eventually left for a public house outside Arundel. In April of that year Ernest Henry Neale became licensee, with Brian Fox following in 1963 and Ian Odde taking over in 1966 until its final closure with sale by auction in 1974. The new owner converted it into a private house with two adjoining garages in place of the beer storeroom. It is now called 'Victory Cottage' and is adjacent to 'Hamilton Cottage', thus preserving an historical linking by name with its neighbour.

Very much regarded by the last licensee as a town pub, it catered for the locals dropping in for a pint and enjoying convivial company in the smoke-filled lounge bar, lit by a small window overlooking King Street, the steep hill running down from London Road with the Cathedral of St Philip Neri at the corner. Entrance was through the door in Nursery Lane, later called New Lane (now Bond Street, probably a corruption of Pond Street), the turning off

17 The Victory *bar before closure.*

to the right from Kings Lane. This was commonly called Panets Pond Lane (now King Street). Going down two steps, with the stairs opposite leading to the living rooms above, and then left, down two more steps, led into the dark wood-panelled surround of the lounge bar with its low-beamed, nicotine-stained brownish ceiling and its layers of old carpet, well-preserved in spilled beer and cigarette ash. Beyond were the private open-plan lounge/dining room and kitchenette.

Locals could crowd round the curved bar, shaped like the stem of an old sea-going tub, with an exit on the far side to get through to the passage at the back that led to a pleasant open-air drinking patio, liquor store and the ladies' and gents', described by those standing at the only window as having the finest panoramic loo-view in the county of the valley towards Chichester.

Over the bar was a portrait of Henry VIII staring down at the drinkers, which at halftime was turned round, and then stared out through four eyes and grinned with two mouths, just to shock those who may have needed sobering up into thinking that they were actually seeing double. This portrait was believed to have been placed there after the Second World War by Mervyn Attwater, a Pathfinder Wing Leader who had completed 61 sorties in Lancasters without a loss and was thus revered and trusted by his crews for his caring leadership qualities. He was Mayor of Arundel in 1968 and 1972. To the right at the entrance was an even smaller room, a snug bar seldom used, with a small interconnecting serving hatch between the bars. It was a free house serving Young's Special Bitter and Whitbread's Tankard and Best Ale.

It ceased trading, after a history of nearly two hundred years, with regulars enjoying a final party in January 1974 with licensee Ian Odde, his wife Gemma and her mother Rosemary Hailes, reported in the *South of England Advertiser* under the heading 'The Victory goes down'.

The White Horse name could be derived from the running horse depicted in the insignia of the Fitzalan family crests. It was sited in old Bridge Street on the 1785 town plan. This is attributed to the occupier William Henty, whose family name was associated with the general business scene in the town and the origin of the Henty Bank. However, subsequent records of the inn in this location cannot be found but, with its position approximating to that of the *General Abercrombie*, conjecture suggests that it could simply have been renamed. Research into the castle archives reveals that a messuage existed called *The White Horse*, lately known as *The Swan*, in High Market Street (High Street since 1766) as it was known in 1756, abutting north-east to the castle ditch on to another old inn called *The Starr*. This property would have been demolished, along with many others, when Charles, 11th Duke of Norfolk, and his successors absorbed that part of the upper High Street, realigned the London Road south of St Nicholas' Church, and built the upper lodge and castle wall as it is today.

However, *The White Horse*, as located on the corner of Tarrant Street and Brewery Hill opposite *The Eagle*, was remembered vividly in the early 1920s by a resident in River Road. She used to run errands for a friend of her mother's, often to the International Stores, before going to school. It was quicker to run up Brewery Hill, passing the back entrance of this old beerhouse. The entrance gates through the archway were frequently open as she ran past and she can remember the 'indescribably horrid smell' emanating from the area. She recalled how she used to hold her breath and pretend that she was climbing a ladder by stepping on the tiny white stones of the narrow footpath opposite, trying not to step on the 'lines'. In the days of the depression after the First World War she remembers seeing unemployed men (probably ex-servicemen) pushing an old perambulator laden with their worldly possessions on the road to Chichester. On their fruitless journeying many of these poor men used the back rooms of *The White Horse* as an overnight refuge.

The fact that Italian organ-grinders, as itinerant bear-keepers toting round their dancing bears to entertain the villagers in the years before the First World War, were a common sight suggests that a few might have survived during the years after the conflict. Rumour has it that a keeper and his bear had stayed in

18 *Site of* The White Horse.

these back quarters. This has been vouched for quite categorically by a resident, who stated that her husband, as a boy, could remember dancing bears coming to Arundel and staying in the outbuildings through the archway in Brewery Hill. Might that 'indescribably horrid smell' be that of the bear itself and its own natural ablutions, confined within unnatural human habitations? The double coach house-type doors give way under a substantial archway to a courtyard beyond, to the right of which is a storeroom with a small iron-grilled window that could safely have housed a caged bear and keeper. To the left is evidence of two unusually large doorways in the back wall, which could have led to stables created beneath the ground floor of the beerhouse itself by the acute downward slope of Brewery Hill. Adjacent is the door giving access to stairs leading to living and sleeping quarters for an innkeeper's family and guests. At the first-floor level a door gives way to a sloping cellar-like storeroom. In the landing wall above, doors give egress from the Tarrant Street ground-floor bar area to the rooms above, which stretch the full width over two floors.

At the front of the building in Tarrant Street, on either side of the main entrance to the public bar at street level, there was front access to extensive cellarage, from which steps led down below the ground floor bars, suggesting that casks would have been delivered via ramps. Residents' memories describe the bar as being along the back wall facing the door, to the right end of which was fixed a brass ornament depicting a man's face smoking a pipe. From it a gas jet was permanently lit, in lieu of matches, for the convenience of the inveterate smokers of the day.

The earliest records show John Elliott seeking reparations in 1807 from the costs of quartering and victualling English troops during the Napoleonic wars. The Arundel Beerhouse Book next records John Thomas Slatter as licensee in 1869, followed in 1870 by Edwin Hopkins and then in April 1874 by George Riddle, who stayed as licensee until November 1886. David Boxall was licensee for a short period only, until the licence was transferred to Frank Slaughter on 13 May 1888. According to the 1891 census Edward Hopkins was resident, though the register of beerhouse keepers named Frank Slaughter as the licensee supplied by Constable's Swallow Brewery. This was confirmed by the 1892 Arundel Directory giving Mr F. Slaughter at *The White Horse*.

The licence was transferred to Richard Neale in November 1901 until 1909, when it was transferred to Arthur George Parsons. He retained the licence for ten years until 1919, during the time of the First World War. These details were confirmed in Pike's Blue Book of 1910-11 and the 1916 Licensees' Minute Book. James Heater became licensee in March 1919 and remained as such until an application for licence renewal was made in 1930 but turned down after referral to the Compensation Authority on the grounds of unsuitable premises and a non-viable business. It was probably due also to the proximity of other near-neighbouring licensed premises in Tarrant Street. Kelly's Directory of 1927 showed the name James Heater as a beer retailer in Tarrant Street.

V

Alehouses

The **Kings Arms**, situated on the corner of Tarrant Street and the extension to Farmers Lane opposite the *Queens Arms*, is reputed to have originated in 1625. It is described as mid-18th-century, with hipped tile roof and red chimneys, two storeys with brick modillion eaves cornice, stuccoed over. The south elevation had two double-hung sash windows with glazing bars on the first floor with a recessed panel between, and the ground floor two mullion and transom windows, one mullion and transom window and one double-hung sash window with glazing bars, all late 19th-century.

The first name associated with the *Kings Arms* was Thomas Strudwick, shown on the 1785 map, followed by Edward Bishop, who had signed the petition of 1807 claiming reparations from the Secretary of War for expenses incurred in accommodating and victualling English troops prior to their embarkation for France to fight Napoleon's forces. The 1824 record of licensees shows William Street as the tenant, confirmed in the auction of 1829, describing the property as having four rooms, a soldiers' room and stabling for six horses. Widow Caroline Hersee occupied the premises in 1836 as the licensee, confirmed in Pigot & Co. in 1839 and the census for 1841, and then in the General Post Office Directory of 1845. Her name was followed by Charles Hatcher, recorded in the census of 1851 as beerhouse keeper. Kelly's Directory of 1855 then referred to both Caroline Hersee and William Shepherd. Although the 1861 census registered Charles Edwards as at the *Kings Arms*, the 1862 GPO Directory showed William Corbett there. The Arundel Alehouses Licence Book records the licensee in 1863 as Owen Overington, who was followed one year later by Matthew Wilson. He became licensee for ten years until Charles Hatcher took over in July 1873 for one year. The 1871 census registered Matthew Wilson as publican at the *Kings Arms* and then only three years later Charles Hatcher.

Following such short-term licence holders came George Redman in July 1874. He remained in charge for fourteen years until the licence was transferred to John Miles on 5 March 1888 for a few months only. Then, on 20 August, Alexander Budgeon became licensee. Both the census of 1881 and Kelly's Directory of

19 *The* Kings Arms.

1882 showed this progression. A ten-year stint by Budgeon, as shown in Kelly's Directory of 1890, registered in the 1891 census and the Arundel Directory of 1892, was followed in rapid succession by James Burtenshaw in May 1897, then temporarily by Alfred Boys in December 1898, Henry Luther Norman in July 1899 and then James Henry Hunt in January 1901. The next record showed in Kelly's Directory of 1905 was John Henry Rogers at the *Kings Arms*, confirmed in Pike's Blue Book 1910-11 with J.H. Rogers and Richard F. Peters in harness at the *Kings Arms* when the licence was transferred in July 1910 to Richard Faulkner Peters.

The next licensee was Andrew Edward Edmunds in October 1913, until John King became licensee in August 1915 until December 1921. Then Henry Charles Prescott took over for a short period until relieved by Frank E. Silverlock in November 1925. He remained until 1940. Entries in Kelly's Directory of 1927 and 1938 show Frank Edward Silverlock at the *Kings Arms Inn*. The Silverlock family stayed in harness with Victor William John Silverlock and Florence Winifred as joint licensees for one year, when John went off to war and Florence Winifred carried on until 1946, when Victor William John returned and continued as licensee until 1959. The Arundel street directory of 1957-8 briefly described the premises as the *Kings Arms Hotel*.

The *Kings Arms* is now described as a pub with beer invariably in a top-rate condition served from two comfortable bars, one with television and dartboard and the other opening on to a higher-level back patio to accommodate the smokers. There are wooden benches outside in Kings Arms Hill itself. Food is served between midday and two o'clock during the week with a Sunday lunchtime treat of ploughman's and a huge chunk of Cheddar best enjoyed in the summer months outside in the sun-drenched patio.

The **Newburgh Arms**, built in the mid-18th century in flint with red brick dressings, stuccoed on the south and west elevations and with a hipped tile roof, was located at the lower end of Tarrant Street on the corner with School Lane. The origin of its name relates to the proximity of the estates belonging to the Earls of Newburgh living in the Elizabethan Slindon House in the nearby village of Slindon. The 5th Earl, Anthony James Radclyffe, was a Jacobite sympathiser and a devout Catholic whose wife Anne Webb spent much of her later life as a widow, encouraged by Catholic emancipation, planning and in her will endowing churches in Chichester and Slindon.

Supplied by Henty & Constable's Ales, Wines & Spirits, the *Newburgh Arms* was a popular dropping-off point for the jockey boys from the castle and char-à-banc (coach) parties from London. Coaches were allowed to park along the footpath to The Slipe, one resident remembering how drunk some of these parties of men became, stripping off and bathing naked in the river. His mother used to help the catering manager, Mrs Beesely, with serving some of the functions. The main door, over which was the licensee's name with the inn sign on the curve of the wall, opened directly into the public bar facing across the room with a dartboard at the far end on the left. The W.C. was outside in the large garden at the back with stables and coach house further along School

20 Newburgh Arms *before closure*.

Lane. To the right of the main door was access to a small snuggery with kitchen quarters behind. Above were living rooms for the landlord and family and a larger room for functions. Access hatches from the footpath enabled beer casks to be unloaded and stored in the large cellar below.

It was unoccupied during the early party of the 19th century when many of the other hostelries were expected to quarter and provide victuals for English troops before they went off to fight the French. Licensee records of 1824 showed William Stone as the landlord, followed by Thomas Cousins in Pigot & Co. 1830, with the 1845 General Post Office Directory and Kelly's of 1855 showing that William Lewis Burrell had taken over. This record was corroborated by the two censuses of 1851 and 1861 and confirmed by the 1862 GPO Directory. The Arundel Alehouse Licence Book registered William Lewis Burrell as licensee in 1863, followed by his widow Charlotte in 1864. The 1871 census and the 1874 GPO Directory showed Charlotte Burrell as a widow, and the 1891 census as the licensed victualler. She retired after being licensee for nineteen years, handing over to her son Arthur in January 1884. He was licensee for a further five years before his premature death brought in the Booker family, with Thomas Booker becoming licensee on 11 November 1889 until July 1896, when he died. Frances Booker, his widow, then became licensee herself in August until 1925, spanning the years of the First World War and the hard times following.

The 1892 Arundel Directory showed Mr T. Booker residing at the '*Newburg Arms*', with the phonetic spelling following its commonplace pronunciation of the day, unlike that of the Earl's family name, which was pronounced as '*New-bruh*'. The advertisement in Kimpton's Popular Guide of 1893 showed the proprietor as T. Booker, but the guide of 1903 then showed that Mrs Booker had taken over as the proprietress. It was described in both editions as the *Newburgh Arms Inn*, offering private apartments, good stabling and coach house, all at moderate prices. This showed that the Bookers had taken over after Mrs Burrell, corroborated by both Pike's Blue Book of 1910-11 and the Licensing Minute Book 1916-35 recording Mrs Frances Booker as the licensee.

The Booker family transferred the licence to Edward Thomas Lock in 1925, who served as licensee until 1940, when his widow Jessie took over for a few months before she handed over to the Puttock family. Archibald Alfred Francis Puttock became licensee in November 1940. Kelly's Directory for 1927 showed Edwin T. Lock at the *Newburgh Arms* public house. Puttock family written records show that they moved in on 13 September 1939, shortly after the announcement by Neville Chamberlain that Britain was at war with Germany. One young girl described the premises as

> a fully licensed house including tobacco. It is a very good house with 5 bedrooms, a large dining room or catering room, kitchen, scullery & sitting room, Saloon & Private Bar, a very large one, Cash Register till. A nice garden with 6 apple trees, 2 stables and garage attached. Own private entrance to backway. Large loft.

The family managed the *Newburgh Arms* through the tough times of the Second World War and the economic struggles after the war with food rationing and fuel shortages.

A number of licensees followed: Peter Frank Lunn in June 1950, Leonard John Chambers in February 1951, Edward Alexander Wood from June 1953 until 1957, Ronald Percy Birch and George Colin Rimmer in November 1957, Jack Bird and Ronald Hugh Castle in May 1958. Before the Puttocks moved out Robert Edward James Barry had become the licensee in May 1959 with wife Elizabeth (Betty) and family. Young Maureen Barry can remember her 21st birthday party and getting married from there too. The next licensee was John Bird, from February 1961 until 1963 when Charles Owen Cox and Joyce Cox took over in February for three years. Dennis Walter Gration became licensee for one year, followed by Patrick George Milford in July 1967. Next came John Martin, licensee from 1970 until 1975 with Eileen, who then went on to run the *Half Moon* at Petworth. The last publicans, until closure in 1982, were Albert (Albie) and June Knight, licensees from 1975. They remember well how quiet Arundel was then, offering bed-and-breakfast accommodation with a garage and car park down School Lane, with Bernie Denyer and wife Maureen (*née* Barry) standing in for them during holiday times until the old alehouse closed and became residential properties.

The **Norfolk Arms**, an imposing Georgian coaching inn with a courtyard entrance, was built in the High Street during 1783-5 under the auspices of the Duke of Norfolk. It is constructed in red brick with rubbed brick voussoirs at ground-floor levels, moulded brick cornices at eaves level above a third floor with a parapet of red brick and grey headers in Flemish bond with ashlar coping masking a hipped slate roof. The Universal British Directory of Trade 1793-8 showed George Blanch as the landlord, having taken over from the *George* when the Duke of Norfolk moved his political meetings there. The *Norfolk Arms* took on a greater significance when, following the passing of the 1785 Paving, Lighting and Cleansing Act, the commissioners appointed to implement the Act were directed to meet at George Blanch's, where rates were fixed not to exceed one shilling in the pound for the High Street, ninepence for Old Market Street and Tarrant Street and fourpence for other streets and lanes. Every inhabitant was bound, under a penalty of 45s., to sweep the pavement from the frontage of his house to the 'channel' or 'kennel' that ran down the centre of each street each day except Sundays, there being no 'sidewalks' in those days.

George Blanch was succeeded by William Balchin, who had added his signature to the 1807 petition claiming recompense from the Secretary of War over the cost of victually and accommodating English troops pending their embarkation to fight the French. He later returned to the *Crown Inn* to manage that establishment. During the period since its building the *Norfolk Arms* was more often closed to the general public than it was open for their

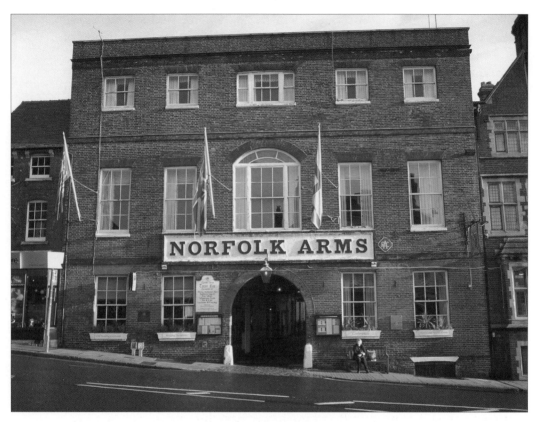

21 *The* Norfolk Arms.

accommodation or, in fact, for any advantage to the tenants who would have benefited from its running. In the course of the year 1812 alone there were no fewer than 12,000 soldiers quartered there during the extended marches along the coast to Portsmouth for transfer across the Channel. The troops were needed by the Duke of Wellington, commander-in-chief of the combined forces gathering in the Low Countries, for the final battle with Napoleon.

There was one man in Arundel who was more than glad to see the back of this vast army departing these shores. Will Quaife was itching to get his inn back from the soldiery that had occupied it to enjoy its comforts rather than face the French across the Channel. In anticipation of the great victory of Waterloo he had advertised in *The Statesman* that he was most respectfully informing the nobility, gentry and commercial travellers, his friends and the public in general that he was re-opening the very commodious and well-known inn, the *Norfolk Arms*. He emphasised that he had recently furnished and fitted everything in a superior style of neatness and comfort and trusted by assiduity and particular attention to merit their favours. 'They may rely,' he stated, 'on being served with the best old wines and Spiritous Liquors: likewise well-aired beds, very convenient Stables and Carriage Houses, Neat Commodious Post Chaises, good Horses and Careful Drivers.' In addition,

William Quaife, under the auspices of the Duke of Norfolk, had added farming facilities to compensate for the heavy demands of the military occupation of the premises.

These facts were confirmed by Mr C. Wright in his 1818 writings published under the title 'History and Description of Arundel Castle' in the section 'Antiquities of Arundel', where he described the *Norfolk Arms* as the principal inn and as being one of the most spacious and commodious houses in this part of the county, possessing every accommodation upon a large scale and having at various times very respectable tenants. He also refers to the Comet Post Coach leaving *The Ship* tavern, Charing Cross, London every morning at seven o'clock and going via Leatherhead, Dorking and Billingshurst for the *Norfolk Arms* and then to Little Hampton and Bognor. The Duke of Norfolk Post Coach set out from *The Dolphin* inn, Little Hampton every Monday, Wednesday and Friday at seven o'clock via Petworth and Guildford and the Earl of Surrey post coach went through Pulborough from Little Hampton every Tuesday, Thursday and Saturday morning at seven o'clock.

Thomas Newman was next to be registered in the 1824 list of licensees, followed by Thomas Cooper. He was the publican named in the 1841 census and shown in the GPO Directory of 1842, and was succeeded by his widow Sarah. Robert Garwood then took over, as shown in Kelly's Directory of 1855 and the GPO Directory of 1862. The 1871 census referred to Robert Garwood as a retired innkeeper who had become mayor for the second time in 1869. The Arundel Alehouse Licence Book records Robert Batchelor Garwood as licensee in 1863, followed in 1876 by Charles Barkshire jnr *in situ*. The 1862 GPO Directory named Charles Barkshire at the *Norfolk Arms* and the censuses of 1881 and 1891 registered him as hotelkeeper for each year. The Arundel Directory of 1892 anticipated new management, naming Charles Barkshire jnr as at the *Norfolk Arms Family and Commercial Hotel*. He advertised in the Salter's Guide for 'Tourists, Families, Travellers, Commercial Gentlemen, and others visiting Arundel. In addition, an Omnibus from the Hotel would meet each train and welcome was given to horses and carriages of every description with excellent and extensive stabling.'

John Nibloe Hare then followed, having moved down from Stranraer in Scotland to buy the lease from the Duke of Norfolk. The licence was transferred to Hare on 13 March 1893. He started the first taxi service in Arundel and used the facilities at the hotel to run a successful transport business, advertising in Kimpton's Guides of 1893 and 1903, until his widow Elizabeth Ann took over, with the licence being transferred to her in November 1900. Record of her stewardship was confirmed in Kelly's Directory of 1905, Pike's Blue Book of 1910-11 and in the Licensing Minute Book of 1912-35. Kelly's Directories of 1927 and 1938 showed that the Hare family still ran the *Norfolk Arms*, with her son George William Favonious in harness from 1922. He was saddled with the name Favonious because his father John Nibloe, registering his son's birth, had won some money on the Derby winner of that year.

During this period running the hotel, the family also ran a small farm off Swanbourne Road, leading to the lake, supplying the *Norfolk Arms* with all its milk, eggs and most of its vegetables and flowers. Young Neil Hare recalls seeing his father, who became mayor on a number of occasions, directing traffic during the General Strike of 1926. He well remembers an event occurring around 1930 when Gaumont British Films moved in to make *The Man from Toronto*, starring Jessie Matthews and Ian Hunter. Most of the action was at Amberley, where Jessie Matthews' temporary home was at the vicarage while the film company made the *Norfolk Arms* their headquarters, much to the delight of a young boy attaching himself to the cameramen while the few internal shots were made in the hotel. He recalls a sewing woman, who was quite an authority on Dickens and taught him much, telling him about the visit of a Red Indian Chief called Big Chief White Horse Eagle. She then said to him, 'Just add *Newburgh Arms* and *Kings Arms* and you have all the pubs in Tarrant Street'.

The licence was transferred away from the Hare family when Alfred James Stanbrook became licensee in August 1946 until May 1949. Cyril Leonard David Beveridge was then licensee for the next six years. In February 1956 the licence was transferred to Vernon Bosley Herbert.

The *Norfolk Arms*, with the name over the impressive archway, is still the largest hotel in Arundel and gives weight to connections between the town and the family at the castle. It is described as a relatively upmarket establishment owned by Forestdale Hotels Limited and is proud to proclaim that the Arundel Society for Prosecuting Villains, Felons and Thieves still hold its annual dinner at the hotel on the Monday nearest to February's full moon – a tradition that dates back some two hundred years. On the left is the town bar, a cosy wood-panelled room with its old prints, paintings and a real fire. Across the courtyard is a smaller hotel bar and comfortable lounge, exuding a quiet, old-fashioned, pre-war charm. In the two centuries since mine host Quaife's reign at the *Norfolk Arms*, the long line of proprietors following has endeavoured to maintain a style and tradition that is essentially part of England and, while emulating these aims, has not sacrificed bodily comfort to satisfy the present demands of hygiene and safety.

The St Mary's Gate, located on the corner of King Street and London Road, was built at the beginning of the 19th century, though it is advertised as originating at the time of Henry VIII and could have been on the site of a former farmhouse. It is constructed of whitewashed brick with a hipped slate roof, brick modillion cornice, in two storeys. During recent redecorating and renewal of the rear wall finish, the revealing of chalk and flint construction indicated that it was not a timbered Tudor-type building. The earliest record of *The St Mary's Gate* was the signature of Robert Glossop signing the 1807 petition for reparations arising from the costs of supplying victuals and accommodation to the nation's troops prior to embarking for the war against Napoleon. He was followed by his widow Elizabeth as licensee in 1824. Next came John Hunt, as recorded

22 The St Mary's Gate Inn.

by Pigot & Co. in 1839, who was succeeded by George Hunt, registered in the census for 1841 as publican at *The St Mary's Gate Inn* and listed in the 1845 GPO Directory.

The 1851 census registered George Hersee as licensed victualler, confirmed in Kelly's Directory of 1855 as at *The St Mary's Gate* and again in the 1861 census and the GPO Directory of 1862. George Hersee continued as innkeeper until he was in his seventies, according to the following two census returns. He was succeeded by his son Alfred James, then in his late thirties, and registered as a licensed victualler. The Arundel Alehouse Licence Book records George Hersee as licensee in 1863, and refers to his death in 1883 and licence transfer to Alfred James Hersee. The licence was briefly transferred to Osborn Bown in November 1887, after which it was transferred back to Alfred Hersee in November 1888. This was confirmed in Kelly's Directories of 1890 and 1905 and the Arundel Directory of 1892.

The next licence reference was a transfer from Alfred James to Ernest Alfred George Hersee in April 1909. Pike's Blue Book of 1910-11 showed that E.A.G. Hersee had succeeded Alfred James. The licence was transferred to Ernest Frank Mustchin in 1913, who was succeeded by Archie George Tee in January 1914. He held the licence into the first three years of the First World War. In April 1917 it was transferred to Thomas Alan Smith for five years until the early 1920s, when Alfred Joseph Glossop became licensee from February 1922 until 1933. Kelly's in 1927 confirms this. Harry Athelstan Webb became licensee in November 1933 until the outbreak of the Second World War, when the husband and wife team of Andrew and Elizabeth Hinson became licensees in November 1939. Elizabeth Hinson was sole licensee for the war years until she handed over the responsibility with the return of Andrew Hinson in February 1951. He held the reins for two years before relinquishing them to Alfred William Richards in

November 1953 for one year. Barbara Mary Lewis, a widow, became licensee with Walter Broome Clark in March 1954. Next came Robert John Smith in August 1957, initially in joint partnership with George Charles Cockman, for eleven years. When Cockman departed in October 1968, Smith continued as sole licensee.

It is described as a traditional English pub serving excellent food, the interior being surprisingly long and roomy with a bar area to the right, a partitioned dining area to the left and a central self-enclosed TV room.

The Black Rabbit is located along Mill Road in the hamlet of Offham/South Stoke on the banks of the River Arun. It was built originally as a row of bare-necessity cottages for labourers working on the Hardham tunnel through the South Downs for the Arun canal development in the 18th century and the railway in the mid-19th century. It is reputed to have been a beerhouse for some two hundred years, though the earliest records found are of John Simpson, the licensee, signing the 1807 petition for reparations. He sought recompense of £16 in lieu of rent on behalf of the inn, then called *The Black Coney* according to records. The auction of 1829 records James Poltick as the tenant and describes the property as having four bedrooms, a soldiers' room, two parlours, a back kitchen, a bar, a dairy and large arched cellar. However, Rodney Walkerley, in his excellent book on Sussex pubs, refers to the early record of John Oliver in

23   The Black Rabbit.

1804 and the fact that the Olivers were there for many years as evidence that can be corroborated with the name of James Oliver reported in Pigot & Co. in 1839 and then in the GPO Directory of 1845.

The census returns for 1871 and 1881 register John Thomas Slatter as publican. This is confirmed by the research conducted by the Slaughter family, from which the Slatters were an off-shoot, that John 'Nib' Slatter was at *The Black Rabbit* until about 1890. Court records of August 1893 show Otto John Henry Behrens as being at *The Black Coney*, while the advertising in Kimpton's Guides of 1893 (Otto Behrens' name being printed as 'Behreus' – the typesetter no doubt misreading 'n' as 'u') offered 'Dancing Saloon, Croquet Grounds, Swings' with 'Luncheons, Dinners & Teas Provided'. It emphasised that wines and spirits of the finest quality were on sale at strictly moderate charges, with the 1903 issue of the Popular Guide reiterating the description by the new proprietor Dan Lee when he took over the licence in September 1895.

Arundel Licence Book records were very sketchy in covering the Offham area. There are alterations in the manuscript to the alehouse name, varying between *The Black Coney* for the years 1940-4 and *The Black Rabbit* when Henry Charles Knight was the licensee between 1945 and 1948, followed by Sam Knight until 1950.

In addition to entertainment on the waterside lawns, which even included archery and broaching barrels of beer, by the start of the 20th century the inn was a favourite destination for char-à-banc and boat trippers. There were two bars – the lounge and the Bunny Bar – together with extensive restaurant catering providing midday and evening meals, now extended into what is advertised as 'probably one of the longest bars in the country'. It now includes an attractive verandah and outside seating and is described as a pub-restaurant, clearly specialising in providing food for visiting families with children, rather than catering for the casual beer drinker.

The **Crown** was a late 15th-century or early 16th-century timber-framed coaching inn with brick and chalk infill and tiled roof, refronted in the 18th century with brick painted white and partially slate-hung behind. It was situated at the bottom of the High Street opposite the old courthouse and the town hall demolished in 1757 to make way for a new Market Square. At the end of the building was an archway for coaches to enter a large courtyard with stabling beyond. There were a number of ground-floor rooms with large fireplaces and narrow staircases to smaller living accommodation rooms above and larger assembly rooms. During the Civil War Parliamentarian troopers stabled their horses on the ground floor and lived above, with little regard to décor or furnishings.

Research into indentures held in the castle archives shows that John Deane occupied the inn in 1764, followed by John Langrish, who leased it to Edward Puttock in 1781 while naming widow Christian Shepherd as having the lease previously. George Blanche purchased the *Crown* in 1787. Other reference

24 *Site of the* Crown.

documents show that the inn was owned by the Shelley family of Michelgrove, with the Baronet of the time using it as surety to raise money to purchase adjacent properties, pending the demolition of older properties that helped to create the Market Square for communal use.

The 1785 town plan shows that John Pell lived there, confirmed in Pigot's directory of 1793-8. John Moorey signed the petition of 1807 declaring what was owed to him as the landlord providing victuals and accommodation to English troops. Reference was made in the *History and Description of Arundel Castle*, written by Mr C. Wright and published in 1818, to the *Crown* being an excellent house, under the management of William Balchin (who had previously been at the *Norfolk Arms*) and having been lately fitted up in the most comfortable manner for the convenience of commercial travellers and the accommodation of families. Improved travel was facilitated by the Cross Post Coach, which ran from the Blue Coach Office, Brighton, every morning at half past nine, arriving at the *Crown* at about twelve o'clock on its way to Portsmouth, while a coach from Portsmouth arrived at about one o'clock and completed the return journey to Brighton at about two o'clock in the afternoon.

In the 1824 register of alehouse keepers Richard Ade was listed. Then, between 1845 and 1855, George Bull was named as the landlord in the Post Office Directory and Kelly's respectively. This was corroborated in the censuses of 1851 and 1861 when, in the latter, George Bull was registered as 'deaf'. The 1862 Post Office Directory showed that William Watts was the landlord, corroborated in the 1863 Arundel Alehouse Licence Book. He was followed in 1864 by his widow Mary Elizabeth, who took over for a three-year period until Henry Randall came down the road from *The Red Lion* in 1867 to be licensee at the *Crown* until his death in 1874. His widow Jane then became the last licensee until closure in 1875, with the declaration in 1871 by the owner Sir John Shelley that his rental contract would be expiring.

In the long struggle between the principal rival political parties of the 18th century, the Whigs were supported by the Shelley family and the Tories by the Dukes of Norfolk. Their respective usage of the *Crown* and the *George* for entertainment, in which the Parliamentary representation of the borough was divided amicably between them, showed how important these old taverns were in the social life of the time. It was the habit of candidates to treat the whole town to wine and punch with competitive carousing in the *Crown* or the *George*, depending upon which candidate arrived first in the town on any one day, though those being supported by the Duke naturally also spent time in the castle and enjoyed its hospitality.

During a Parliamentary Election in 1735 when Sir John Shelley and Colonel Lumley were sitting as MPs, the Duke had sought to influence the election of mayor based on political considerations, the mayor being the returning officer who could decide who had or had not the right to vote. This influence subsequently resulted in Sir John Shelley losing his seat at the General Election of 1742. Though the likely reason was the general decline of popularity of the Walpole government of the day, the possibility of a mayor supporting the candidate opposing the sitting member should not be discounted entirely.

Not only was unconcealed financial bribery rife at the time, but entertainment on such a lavish scale would also have had a salutary effect on the result of a General Election, the campaigns for such continuing over a number of years. Parliament was suddenly dissolved in September 1774 and a proclamation made by King George III demanding a new parliament to sit after elections were held throughout the country. As a result, two MPs, one from each side of the political divide, were nominated by the returning officer, the mayor John Tompkins, as described by Dr G.W. Eustace in his history of Arundel and the castle.

The competition between these two political factions was brought to an end at the beginning of the next century and with it the need for extensive entertaining of candidates. The Borough of Arundel had returned two MPs since 1295 but with the Reform and Boundary Bill of 1832 the borough lost half of its representation and would have had it removed altogether had there been sanctioned the proposal to annex part of the parish of Littlehampton within the Rape of Arundel, and thus convert Arundel Borough to a mere nomination borough for a Peer of Parliament. However, it was not sanctioned due to the protests and petitions by the mayor and corporation against the boundary changes. When the Boundary Act received Royal Assent on 11 July 1832 the ancient limits of the Borough of Arundel were left undisturbed.

These events could well have contributed to the decline in usage of these old inns as centres of hospitality providing elaborate dinners and high-class accommodation. The more likely reason for their eventual closure was the emergence of the newer, more commodious, *Norfolk Arms*, built under the auspices of the Duke himself.

The *Crown Inn* was also the regular meeting place for the Arundel Society for Prosecuting Villains, Felons and Thieves from 1776 to 1829, after which date the minute book shows that meetings had taken place from 1830 to 1884 at the *Norfolk Inn*, from 1885 to 1958 at the *Norfolk Hotel* and from 1959 to the present at the *Norfolk Arms*. During this time there were two records of trials being held at the Horsham Assizes significant to the ale and beerhouse history of Arundel. One was concerning the stealing of wine from watchmaker Robert Burfield, who lived in the High Street near the *Norfolk Arms*, in 1796, and the other was stealing money from the counting house at the Eagle Brewery in 1878. Although the last survivors of a volunteer police force, common in country districts before the establishment of a national police force, the society has every intention of continuing its annual dinner and maintaining records of each meeting in their minute book.

With Georgian façade restoration covering the ancient timber framework and then subsequent Victorian additions, the era of the *Crown* ended in the late 19th century when it became residential, with shop premises on the ground floor and the courtyard behind losing its stables to become a car park.

The Dolphin/The Bridge Hotel was shown on the 1785 map in Queen Street, adjacent to the River Arun bridge, with George Picknett and James Champion's names alongside the building, confirming that it was at least of 18th-century origin. Edward Stallard was the next licensee. George Young was the licensee in 1824, followed by Edmund Forrest in 1834, who died within a year and was succeeded by his widow Rhoda in running *The Bridge Commercial Hotel*. In the 1851 census she was described as a former innkeeper. The 1841 census and the GPO directory for 1845 showed Phillip Sensier as the occupier. He was followed by Henry Peters, as recorded in the 1851 census and Kelly's Directory for 1855. The next occupier, as shown in the 1861 census, was James Parris at *The Bridge Inn*, with the GPO Directory of 1862 showing him still there. The Arundel Alehouse Licence Book registers James Parris as licensee in 1863, followed by George Tilley from 1864 until 1879, when his widow Annie took over in August. The 1871 census showed that George Tilley was the innkeeper, but his widow Annie was recorded in the 1891 census as hotel keeper – she was after all thirteen years younger than he was and George was nearly seventy in 1871. She managed the premises until 1891, during which period she renamed it *The Bridge Hotel*.

In November 1891 the licence was transferred to Lewis Gordon Burrell, son of Arthur Burrell, whose family had managed the *Newburgh Arms*. Lewis Gordon was also proprietor of Burrell's Refreshment and Dining Rooms in the Market Square. The Arundel Directory of 1892 confirmed that Mr L.G. Burrell was at *The Bridge Hotel*. Kimpton's Popular Guide to Arundel dated 1893 advertised *The Bridge Hotel* with L. Gordon Burrell as the proprietor, and the one for 1903 suggested that he was still there and it was advertised as *The Bridge Family Hotel*. Burrell had in fact died in the winter of 1902, when there was a temporary transfer of the licence to Richard Willard, from whom the licence was then transferred in March 1903 to Mary Ann Burrell, Lewis's widow, who held it for two years before relinquishing it to a spinster, Miss Louisa Mary Challen, in November 1905. She held it for nearly ten years. The licence then went to Ernest Frank Mustchin in January 1914, who handed it over to his wife Ellen Kate in January 1917. She kept going through the remaining years of the First World War until 1920, when the licence returned to her husband Ernest Frank Mustchin from May 1920 until the late 1930s.

Frank Mustchin's missing years from 1917 to 1920 are a puzzle. It could be suggested that, since he had survived the war period, he could have been a prisoner-of-war and that his repatriation had taken its toll until 1920. Alternatively, he could have suffered war wounds that required considerable recovery time before he could take on the burden of being a publican again. Whatever it was, he must have been a fit man to be so long in harness and managing the hotel until the late 1930s. The joint licensees in 1936 were then Frank and Mary Osborne, with Mary Osborne taking over solo from 1938 until 1947, spanning the traumatic years of the Second World War. The licence was then transferred to Wilfred Ingham Briggs in September 1947, who, after twelve years, handed over to the joint partnership of Roland Percy Birch and Victor Henry Manning in August 1959. Manning left the partnership and Robert James Donnelly joined Ronald Birch in December 1961. This partnership continued until 1967 when Peter Fish became sole licensee in March for one year, until Brenda Barbara Webb became licensee in April 1968.

The building was a typical coach house, with an archway from Queen Street leading into a large area behind that catered for horses and carriages of every description. It was described as a hotel, with spacious dining saloon, private sitting rooms, verandah and balcony, splendidly situated overlooking the River Arun, with good stabling, carriages for hire and billiards. The advertisement in Kimpton's Guide for 1903 was not quite as detailed, describing it as a hostelry providing every accommodation at moderate terms, beautifully situated, fronting the castle, overlooking the River Arun and commanding delightful views of the surrounding country. It again emphasised that the one special facility being offered was 'Billiards', which, presumably, was the rage at the turn of the 20th century. It also confirmed that, in 1903, 'It was lighted throughout by Electricity' – a unique feature that was highly innovative and would attract business to Arundel, since many places in the town were still gas-lit even after the Second World War.

The early building with its attractive features and ivy-covered walls survived, a relic commemorating the pace of the days before the motor car, until the 1930s, when the road bridge was rebuilt in 1935. The engineers at the time, in order to construct support piles on the riverbed itself, diverted the river via a coffer dam without calculating the force of this constricted flow with tidal surge and its effect on the river's south bank. The erosion of the bank also undermined the foundations of the hotel, which slowly collapsed into the river, taking with it the gardens and conservatory tearoom. In fact, the staff then in attendance

25 *Old* Bridge Hotel *before 1935*.

26 *New* Bridge Hotel *after 1935*.

can recall with amazement how they opened a door into this area and witnessed an unexpected panoramic view of upper Arundel.

Needless to say, the rest of the building had to be demolished and a new 20th-century *Bridge Hotel* built in its place. Older residents remember the original hotel with some affection and, as they walked in from the Fitzalan Road side, via the Swallow Brewery, how attractive the inside looked when viewed from the door under the archway. Rodney Walkerley, in his 1966 book *Sussex Pubs*, described the replacement building as a modern Georgian-style house with rooms that were high and spacious, carpeted and comfortable in the modern manner. It was a Friary Meux house, serving Double Diamond and Watney's Red Barrel. There was a big lounge bar, a snack bar and a restaurant. They did teas at a fixed price and there was a garden for children. The new *Bridge Hotel* was demolished in 1988 to make way for retirement homes.

The Eagle, as it is now known, was located on the site of the 'Malt & Brewhouse', as shown on the 1785 map, halfway along Tarrant Street on the corner with Brewery Hill, the early footpath leading down to the river. Originally licensed as a beerhouse by John Burton and known as the *Brewers Arms*, its history as *The Eagle* public house only really started with the first entry in the Arundel Alehouse Licence Book. It was relicensed as an alehouse in May 1889 with William Miles, the licensee at the *Brewers Arms*, transferring it to Otto Behrens, who became the first licensee of *The Eagle* in 1889. Kelly's Directory of 1890 showed Otto Thomas Henry Behrens at *The Eagle*. This was confirmed in Salter's Visitors' Guide advertisement for 'The Eagle Commercial Inn, with Every Accommodation for Beanfeast Parties and Excursionists (Luncheons, Dinners, & Teas Provided) with Good Stabling and Official Quarters for Cyclists' Touring Club, all under the proprietorship of Otto Behrens.'

The licence was then transferred to Charles Southby Arbery on 2 March 1891. This was confirmed in the 1891 census, which registered Charles S. Arbery (with wife Elizabeth) as a licensed victualler, and the 1892 Arundel Directory's entry of C.S. Arbery at *The Eagle Inn*. This stewardship was an ongoing one, with Kelly's Directory of 1905 and Pike's Blue Book of 1910-11 showing C.S. Arbery as licensee. Charles Arbery was also remembered as a pillar of the two-hundred-year-old Arundel Cricket Club, not only as a player, but also as one who saw to it that the team had a wicket fit for their skills by spending hours each week, with his penknife, taking out offending daisies and plantains from the sacred turf as well as supervising the preparation of the ground as a whole. Also among the better-known players at the time were E.T. Norris, a partner of Lambert & Norris Brewery, and Archie Jupp (see p.57).

The next licensee was Frank Thomas Washington in April 1911. There was a temporary transfer in October 1915 to Roger George Martin, who became licensee for a short time before volunteering for the front and leaving his wife, Frances Esther Martin, in charge in January 1917. After the First World War, Roger George Martin was registered again as licensee in May 1920, though

27   The Eagle.

Kelly's Directory of 1927 still recorded Frances Esther Martin as the licensee. She was no doubt one of those war-tough widows who had carried on relentlessly even after the return of their men folk. Her husband had been renowned as a Boer War veteran. The next licensee was Frederick William Arlett in March 1930, who stayed on until just before the Second World War. Then the Martin family returned in 1938 with joint licence-holders Percy Edgar Martin and Alice Emma Martin. Alice Emma took over on her own one year later, handing the licence to Gerald Arthur Atkinson in 1943. She remained until 1954, when in November Kenneth James Wesson became licensee for the next four years.

A wartime incident brought notoriety to *The Eagle* when a serviceman, following heavy drinking there, broke into 'Knocker' Knowles's old junk shop in Bung Row, the row of cottages in Tarrant Street opposite the pub, and murdered Knowles's elderly daughter Amelia, subsequently being caught, sentenced and hanged at Wandsworth Prison.

The Eagle has been refurbished over the years and takes its place as one of the surviving pubs from a bygone era, now described as 'trendy-traditional' with its largish L-shaped interior comfortably provided with a real fire at one end. In addition to its selling alcoholic refreshment it offers comprehensive catering in the cellar restaurant.

The Mile House/The White Swan on the Chichester Road, one mile out of Arundel, started life as an early 18th-century brick-built tiled house, constructed in the form of an L, with a small low-walled garden in front dominated by a large oak tree. In its original form it was described as having two bars, both approximately 12ft square, one facing south and the other west, each with a fireplace. On one side were a four-stall stabling, coach house, tool shed and two pigsties and runs, with an outside closet. The long uphill pull from Arundel to Portsmouth frequently necessitated changing horses on arrival at the inn.

Early records show Joseph Jupp as licensee in 1893, when it was known as *The Swan* at Tortington. Later the name became *The White Swan*, this being confirmed in the Arundel Alehouse Licence Book in 1912. The licence transferred to Frances Jupp in February 1916. No specific record has been found with any other names for the old alehouse, which was known colloquially as *The Mile House*, being that distance from the town centre. Frances Jupp kept going as licensee until widower Archie Joseph Jupp took over from May 1930 until 1963. Francis Jupp (Fanny) was recorded in the Licensing Minute Book 1916-35 and Kelly's Directory of 1927. The well-famed Archie Jupp was the last male publican, an ex-First World War soldier of unique character, remembered as captain of the Arundel Cricket Club until the outbreak of the Second World War but earlier as the up-and-coming fast bowler who was largely responsible for reclaiming the ground from weeds and molehills and waist-high grass.

The Jupp family had occupied the old inn for nearly a hundred years. Their farming land was nearby and they were responsible for the brick yard across the road. During *The Swan*'s ownership as a free house by the Duke of Norfolk he had promised not to sell it while 'Juppy' was still alive. Following the death of the licensee in 1963 it was sold by auction in 1964, covenants on the sale ensuring that no public or private lunatic asylum, convalescent home, public garage or petrol station could be built thereon.

28 The Mile House – *as remembered.*

29 *Bar of* The White Swan *about 1950.*

30 The White Swan Hotel.

On the sale specification it was described as having a central entrance door leading into a lounge hall with rear door to the garden and a snug, 10ft by 6ft 6in, with fireplace. From the lounge a door to the right went into the public bar, 17ft by 10ft. Arundel residents remember it as being ill-lit by candles and two gas lamps on the side wall, the latter fed from a shilling-in-the-slot-meter that frequently gave up, throwing the room into semi-darkness, until replenished. The zinc-covered oak-plank bar was on the dividing wall with the kitchen behind and the till at the end, from which the shillings materialised to light up the room again. Well remembered too was the behaviour of the landlord, whose irascible nature frequently got the better of him, particularly when the till and its coin contents went flying over the floor.

It is still affectionately remembered as 'Juppy's', with its sawdust-covered floor, scrubbed pine tables and the tree in the front garden. It survived until the present *White Swan Hotel* was built round the old cottage in the 1970s, demolishing the coach house, taking over the retail function and converting to electric lighting.

The Old Ship succeeded to its title after the demise of *The Ship*, shown on the 1785 map as being near the corner of Poor House Hill (now Park Place) and Old Market Street. It is described as an early 19th-century two-storey double-fronted building of beach flint, brick dressings, pitched slate roof and double-hung sashes with glazing bars. Residents of Arundel have described it as 'small and cosy', having a single entrance door off King Street with a door to the right leading to the public bar and its three tables and chairs, with the bar itself set at a right-angle to the window. This led beyond to a smaller room at the back with a dartboard, and a further door off the street down an alley next to the bakery gave way to the jug and bottle hatch to the bar. From the main entrance another door led left to the bar parlour.

The 1824 Register of Licensees showed that Edward Puttock and George Constable owned *The Old Ship*, with Edward Elliott as the landlord until he was succeeded by John Searle from 1827. He died in 1839, when his widow Elizabeth took over until 1844. William Elliot replaced her, but stayed for only three years, when Edward Overington became licensee. His widow Elizabeth survived him to be landlady until she was into her mid-seventies, with Richard Blackman taking over in November 1885 until 1896, when William Edward Glossop became licensee on 20 January. This was recorded later in Pike's Blue Book of 1910-11. He was nicknamed 'Rush' Glossop, due to his general slowness at serving and attending to customers, and stayed until 1927. He was followed by Walter Poat, with the Duke of Norfolk as the owner. Walter Poat, with wife Emma, was the licensee prior to and following the Second World War, until he handed over to Ernie and Flora Street in December 1948 with the ownership changing to the Friary Brewery. Changes were made to the building, too, with a third window inserted at first-floor level above a new doorway, together with a new inn sign bracket. An extended ground-floor window to the right of the door

31   The Old Ship.

with three narrower integral double-sash windows replaced the older window and the entire facing was whitewashed. The original bracket ended up on the wall of Herbie Smith's antique shop when he bought the old telephone exchange in Tarrant Street. It then became Tricot's gown shop, next to the Muse Café that at one time was the stables and coach house for the Arundel Brewery, a name synonymous with the Eagle Brewery located down Brewery Hill opposite.

The Streets stayed until 1955, handing over to Alan and Mary Spearman for two years until they were replaced by a widow, Florence (Flo) Pecksen, who was followed by Cecil C. Wood. He remained for six years, with Henry Montague Page succeeding him for just over a year. James and Iris Wiltshire took over for a short spell and John and Kathleen Farr became the last publicans until closure in 1979, with the new owner converting it into two private houses.

The Railway Inn/The Railway Hotel, was built on the Arundel side of the railway bridge in 1860, separating it from the parish of Lyminster. The *West Sussex Gazette* of 3 August 1865 gives rise to some confusion over the name by reporting that a person charged with stealing a dead hare was seen at *The Railway Inn* but, in reporting another misdemeanour, a Mr Rewell was named as the landlord of *The Railway Hotel* as witness to an alleged felony. Though this helped to confirm who was licensee at the time it did not establish the correct name of the establishment itself. William Atfield was the next licensee, as recorded in the 1881 census. The Arundel Directory of 1892 showed Mr Bill Tee at *The Railway Inn*. This was confirmed by the Arundel Alehouse Licence Book, which showed William Granger Tee as licensee before he died in 1893. He was followed by his widow Lilly Ann for one year before she too passed away. Her son Thomas, as executor to her will, then arranged transfer of the licence to another widow, Jane Hersee. Jane survived three years as licensee from May 1895 until 1898 when the executor to her will, John Henry Bird, ensured transfer of the licence to Henry Edward Elston on 8 August 1898. Henry lasted not three years, dying in May 1901 to be followed by his widow Annie in June, who promptly transferred the licence to George Richard Coleman in August, and it was renewed annually until 1904. The next licensee was Edward Charles Peake in November of that year, who successfully carried on until 1931. Pike's Blue Book of 1911 showed E.C. Peake as licensee at *The Railway Hotel*, confirmed in Kelly's Directory of 1927 as Ernest Charles Peake. Tabitha Ellen Peake, Edward's widow, then took over.

Local residents recall that in 1950 the publican was Tom Finch and at that time the name had not changed from *The Railway Hotel*, as supplied by Friary, who had taken over from Henty & Constable's Swallow Brewery when it closed in 1930. By 1953 the publican was a Mr Searle, who had been a bus driver. By 1970 it had become *The Welcome Inn* and had been sold to Sidney Clinch, who renamed it *The Golden Goose*, when it sported a beautiful brown carpet into which had been woven a golden goose motif. The wrought iron décor above the bar incorporated a flying golden goose. The next landlord was John Hunter, who had been a hotel owner in the New Forest, followed by Jim and Elisabeth Lindsey, who set out to cater for the local clientele and build up a friendly relationship with the neighbours. It was next sold to Michael Cringe, who initiated the first extension with the introduction of the Sussex Bar. At that time the old barn behind the hotel had been removed and a car park put in its place.

Then came Mr and Mrs Metcalfe from the Isle of Wight, whose daughters unsuccessfully endeavoured to turn it into a nightclub for a younger clientele. Two more publicans followed in quick succession, turning the hotel into a pub and restaurant complex until David and Sue Haines arrived to concentrate more on a bed-and-breakfast establishment and on functions and wedding receptions. They added a conservatory and an attractive garden with a larger car park to the railway station side of the available land. One significant gesture to good neighbourliness was to ensure that any licence extensions never went beyond midnight and car parking alongside the hotel adjacent to immediate properties was curtailed. After a somewhat chequered career, *The Railway Inn* emerged under the new name of *The Arundel Park Hotel*. The present owner describes the premises as an independently run family hotel giving a welcome to residents and non-residents, catering for special occasions, weddings, parties and meetings in the restaurant function room and enabling patrons to enjoy a

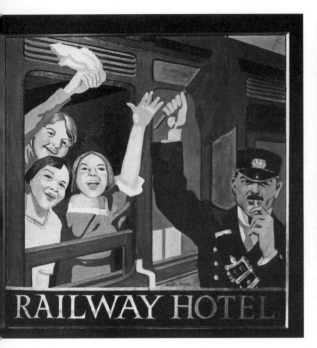
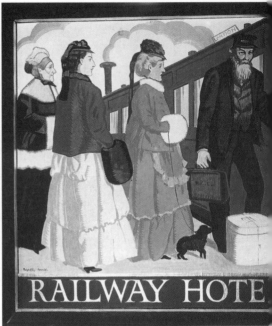

32 The Railway Hotel *inn sign, 1926.*

33 The Golden Goose *bar (*The Railway Hotel*)*.

34 The Arundel Park Hotel *(The Railway Hotel).*

coffee in the friendly atmosphere of the conservatory or simply to relax in the garden overlooking the Sussex countryside.

The Red Lion, a late 18th-century brick-fronted inn with slate pitched roof, is not specifically named on the High Street in the 1785 plan, although it was occupied by John Gilbert. An indenture held in the castle archives, dated 1793, names 'John Gilbert with Richard Plummer on Mincing Lane abutting the *Crown Inn* then privately owned by George Blanch'. Today, these two properties are separated by a smaller later property built on the land between that extends behind to the passageway exiting into Tarrant Street by *The Heart in Hand* (now a shop) and a licensed restaurant. Earlier records in the castle archives refer to Minsinge Lane, on which a messuage formerly called *The Red Lion and Anchor* (near John Walder's house – not identified) was named. Against a date 1793 there is a further reference to *The Red Lion* with the words '*and Anchor*' as having being dropped.

Early occupation records start with the Universal British Directory of Trade of 1793-8 naming William Souter as the landlord of *The Red Lion*. He was followed by John Pullin, the signatory to the 1807 Petition to the Secretary of War seeking reparations. Licensee records of 1824 show Richard Parrish as landlord and for 1833 William Morley, who was succeeded on his death in 1836 by his widow Mary, as confirmed by Pigot & Co. in 1839. William Souter then took over the running in the next year, as shown in the 1841 census and the GPO Directory of 1845. He was succeeded by Henry Dyer, registered as a licensed victualler in the 1851 census and confirmed in Kelly's Directory of 1855. Although a comparatively young man, he was succeeded by a younger Henry Randall, recorded in both 1861 and 1871 census returns at *The Red Lion*.

The Arundel Alehouse Licence Book registers Henry Randall as the licensee from 1863, who in 1867 went off to help at the *Crown*, with the next licensee at *The Red Lion* being Edward Witham. The census return for 1871 showed the fifty-year-old Edward Witham registered at the same address with his wife Lucy, confirmed in the GPO Directory of 1874. Edward Witham died in 1878 and the licence was taken over by his widow.

The next census ten years later showed that Lucy Witham was still a widow and the licensed victualler at the age of fifty-nine. She then handed over to her son Thomas in 1888, whose sudden death during the winter of 1888 was recorded in the Arundel Licence Book. Lucy Burch temporarily took over as licensee in January 1889, suggesting that Lucy Witham had married a Mr Burch. John Ellwood became licensee on 4 March 1889, shown as John E. Ellwood by the 1891 census as licensed victualler at *The Red Lion*. He was brother to Mary Jane, who was now married to James Stevens, licensee at *The Swan Inn* just down the road towards Town Quay. As proprietor, Ellwood advertised in Kimpton's Guides of 1893 and 1903 that *The Red Lion Commercial Inn*, Ancient Order of Foresters (A.O.F.) no. 2322, in The Square, Arundel was selling Constable's Swallow Brewery's celebrated Arundel ales and stout. In addition, the inn provided luncheons, dinners and teas and emphasised 'Every Accommodation for Cyclists'. Pike's Blue Book of 1910-11 recorded J.E. Ellwood at *The Red Lion*.

A connection with the family that had links with other taverns in the town was established when May Charlotte, sister to Frederick (Nip) Slaughter (who with wife Sylvia ran the *General Abercrombie* in Queen Street), married George Bosworth and came to *The Red Lion* in May 1917. In this period around the First World War, William Calcutt was recorded as licensee in 1919 until 1921, when May Charlotte Bosworth took over as licensee until 1940. Kelly's Directories of 1927 and 1938 confirm that she was in this role. They also suggest that husband George had not returned from the First World War to resume his post in 1919, when William Calcutt became licensee.

The early Henty & Constable alehouse, with its central door and ground-floor bay windows on either side, was demolished in 1935. Adjoining was a tobacconist's shop with a larger bay window for displaying its wares, above which were four double-sash windows with glazing bars giving first-floor accommodation for the publican and family. The vacant space thus created was vividly remembered by a five-year-old boy living opposite, as he watched *The Red Lion* of 1937 being built. This building was faced with red brick under a red clay-tiled hip-roof with three pairs of double-hung glazing-barred sash windows, two pairs over the alehouse and one over the adjacent shop. The ground floor comprised two-paired glazing-barred sash windows on either side of a false door. A left-hand door gave access to customers' lavatories and a door on the right entrance to the bar. Next to it was the adjacent shop with its distinctive window. Figure 37 clearly shows, on the painted wall of the adjacent building, the line of the old pitched roof and chimneystack.

35 The Red Lion *before its rebuild*.

36 *Arundel High Street showing* The Red Lion *(as above)*.

37 The Red Lion *rebuilt in 1937.*

Originally the drinking area surrounded a two-sided bar with a dining room to the left, since which time it has been changed to increase the dining area. It was described as a friendly, homely, unpretentious town pub with a dartboard and decorated with old *Vanity Fair* prints depicting caricatures of jockeys. One feature preserved was the hanging 'bush', displayed as a hop flower and made of painted carved wood, together with the inn sign on the bracket outside. The Arundel street directory of 1957-8 briefly described the premises as *The Red Lion Hotel*.

The next licensee, spanning the years of the Second World War, was Robert Clarence Batt. He was followed by Reginald Ernest Bristow from August 1951 until 1957, during which time Friary, Holroyd & Healie's Brewery took over in February 1955. The next licensee was John Richard Holloway from August 1957 until 1962 when Walter Donald Hart became licensee. Valentine Saxby Savigear was next in April 1966 and then came Trevor Keith Lucas in December 1968. Charles Patrick Rogers was licensee from 1974 until 1983. Derek and Sara Hanson, bringing up their young family, took over the licence until Derek decided to retire in April 2005, handing over to Chris Goy. They turned to renovating the space between *The Red Lion* and the *Crown* and converted the building into a coffee shop, trading as 'Grounds'.

The name of **The Swan** has appeared in indentures, dated mid- to late 18th century and held in the castle archives, in relation to a messuage called *The White Horse* and lately known as *The Swan* in High Market Street (called High Street after 1766), abutting north-east to the castle ditch. Other indentures refer to *The Swan* in the lane leading to the water mill (Mill Lane) that ceased functioning as such in 1698.

However, *The Swan,* a mid- to late 18th-century brick building with stucco finish and hipped tiled roof with dormer windows on the third floor, the west end of its extension being beach flint, clunch and random Pulborough stone with red-brick chaining, is now located on the corner of the High Street opposite the old Henty Bank House facing Town Quay. Early records show a 1759 conveyance jointly between Edward Arnop, a wealthy Petworth butcher, William Mitford esquire, gentleman of Tillington House, and George Lane, coal merchant of Arundel. *The Swan* is shown on the 1785 town plan with the name William Lucas on the site, confirmed in the 1793-8 Universal British Directory of Trade & Commerce.

Next named is John Brooks, who signed the 1807 Petition claiming reparations from the Secretary of War for expenses incurred in accommodating and victualling English troops. The 1824 register of licensees showed John Simpson as publican. The 1829 auction refers to Stephen Challen as the tenant at will at *The Swan Inn* and as having stabling for nine horses. He was followed by Richard Lillywhite, registered in the 1841 and 1851 census returns as the licensed victualler, a sprightly 77-year-old who was succeeded by Charles Edwards as recorded in the 1855 Kelly's Directory. Afterwards came the elderly William Baker, registered in the 1861 census as innkeeper at *The Swan*.

The Arundel Alehouse Licence Book records Elizabeth Ellwood, a widow, as the licensee in 1863, confirmed by the 1871 census showing her, then 56 years old, as registered innkeeper at *The Swan Inn*. Also registered were two daughters, Elizabeth (26) and Mary Jane (18), living with her as assistant innkeepers, and a son, John Ellwood (16), a trainee printer, with James Stevens (16) as lodger. Young James was two years younger than Mary Jane and must have been quite a stunner because they were soon married and running the place together, to the relief, no doubt, of Mary Jane's mother. The Arundel Licence Book shows that Elizabeth Ellwood senior died in 1881, handing over to her son John, who then arranged transfer of the licence to James Stevens. The censuses of 1881 and 1891 showed James Stevens registered as the licensed victualler at *The Swan Inn* with wife Mary Jane Stevens and offspring Archibald (5), Lionel F.T. (2) and Gordon Harry (under one month). Mary Jane's brother John had by this time moved to *The Red Lion* and was registered as the licensed victualler there. The Arundel Directory of 1892 showed Mr J. Stevens at *The Swan*, with Mr J.E. Ellwood at *The Red Lion* up the High Street on the left next to the *Crown*.

A brass sign engraved 'James & Mary Stevens 1870-90' was on display within the inn at the time. The Arundel Licence Book shows that Mary Jane, by then a widow, had become licensee in 1899. It is recorded that James Stevens had died

38 The Swan *in the late 19th century.*

after being hit on the head by a cricket ball. Kimpton's Guide to Arundel of 1903 advertised *The Swan Inn* as giving 'Good Accommodation for Travellers and Cyclists with Beds and Stabling, Wines and Spirits of Superior Quality at terms on application'. No reference was made to ales or beers, implying that they were offering hotel-type accommodation. In addition, the guide mentioned that 'Beanfeasts and other Parties [were] Catered for', indicating that there were facilities for the preparation and presentation of comprehensive menus. Mrs Stevens was advertised as the proprietress. The Arundel Licence Book next records that Alice Mansell Boswell, also a widow, had taken over the licence in November 1916, continuing throughout the First World War until early 1919. The Licensing Minute Book dated 1916-35 shows Mary Jane Stevens' name on the list, followed in 1919 by Alice Boswell.

At that time, records also show that William Calcutt was licensee from February 1919 until September 1925, when he was replaced by the next licensee, William Withall. During this confused period, William Calcutt's name also appeared in licence records as licensee at *The Red Lion*, this fact confirming the relationship between the two alehouses in which the various managing families were closely interconnected and no doubt would have helped one another. Kelly's Directories of 1927 and 1938 show William Jason Withall as the landlord until the outbreak of the Second World War. His widow Lillian became licensee in 1943 until June 1953 when Leonard Ernest Hammond took over for two years until succeeded briefly by Albert Walter Fluter in February 1955. Tamplin's Brewery of Brighton became the owners in May 1955 when Anthony Allan John Jex and his wife Anita became the general managers. Anita became sole licensee in April 1963 for five years, relinquishing the licence to Alfred Lawrence Pyott in March 1968.

The early building possessed a courtyard at the back with stabling, accessible through gates, for horses and coaches. This part has now long gone, with a new road giving access into the Crown Yard car park and two rows of small shops. The adjacent High Street shop was absorbed into the main premises, which were extended rearwards to utilise redundant space behind. In addition, a further dormer window was added to overlook the High Street. During work on the attic ducting a piece of old timber was found, on which was scribbled 'George F Weller 1898'. Weller is an old Arundel name and, in the mid-19th century, Weller & Kendall traded from a builder's workshop in River Road. At the entrance from the High Street the ground floor is separated into a large tap-room bar to the left, with 19th-century oak flooring and pine paneling, and a more formal lounge bar restaurant area to the right and rear with the old pub sign from around 1750 on display at the far wall. Photographs of the hotel as it was in former times are displayed at the side entrance lobby

39 The Swan Hotel.

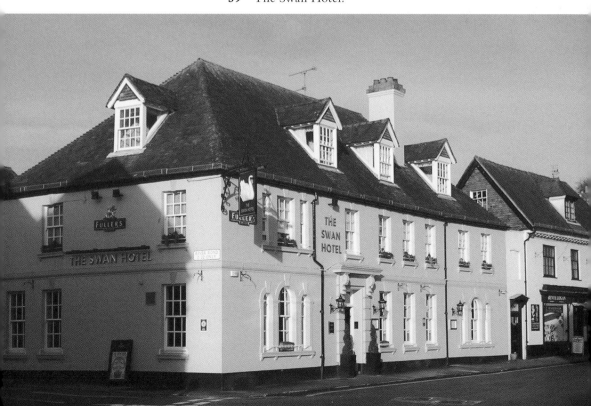

and many that commemorate Sussex sporting events are round the walls of the restaurant and lounge area.

The Arundel street directory of 1957-8 briefly described the premises as *The Swan Inn*. *The Swan Hotel* is now described as a Grade II-listed hotel, with the brewery name 'Fuller's' adorning the wall facing the Town Quay near the inn sign.

The final alterations were carried out by Ken and Diana Rowsell, licensees in the 1980s, when the shop next door was incorporated to provide the extra bedrooms and restaurant space. As a hotel it boasts 15 bedrooms, all with *en suite* toilet facilities (bathroom or shower), tea and coffee-making, TV and Wi-Fi facilities for personal computers. In addition, there are two executive suites. It has a warm friendly atmosphere with an old-world charm. The present licensees and general managers are Stacey Reynolds and Jim Dobbins, responsible to the independent family brewers Fuller's, established in 1845.

The Wheatsheaf, an early 18th-century building with grey brick headers and red brick dressings with a hipped tiled roof, was located on the south side of Old Market Street (now Maltravers Street). It is shown on the 1785 map as the residence of George Puttock (maltster and brewer) with no record of its conversion into an inn. Records show John Hersee as the landlord when he signed the 1807 petition for reparations of costs arising from the Napoleonic wars. He was listed in the licensees' register of 1824-9. The 1829 auction described the property as having two front sitting rooms, a bar, a spacious club room and very

40 *The sign of* The Wheatsheaf, *1880.*

41 *Site of* The Wheatsheaf.

large cellars, after which time it appeared to have been unoccupied, according to Pigot & Co. in 1839. The GPO Directory of 1845 showed John Turner as landlord, followed by James Lashley, as recorded by Kelly's Directory of 1855. The Arundel Alehouse Licence Book records Frederick Lucas as licensee in 1863 until 1876, when Alan Blackman took over. The GPO Directory of 1862 showed that Fred Lucas was a beer retailer in Maltravers Street, and the 1861 and 1871 censuses show Frederick Lucas at *The Wheatsheaf*. Blackman died in 1883 and, on 14 January, Samuel Hyatt Morgan became licensee.

This was corroborated by an 1880s photograph showing an inn sign on the right-hand side of Maltravers Street looking towards the castle, with a wheatsheaf image and the publican's name, Samuel H. Morgan, on it. The 1881 census named Samuel Morgan as the licensed victualler, followed by the 1891 census specifying Samuel Hyatt Morgan as the innkeeper. The Arundel Directory of 1892 confirmed that, in Maltravers Street, Mr S. Morgan was at *The Wheatsheaf Inn*. The next record from the licence book records S.H. Morgan as dying at the end of 1904. The licence was transferred in January 1905 to Edward Leggett and John Bennett jointly and then went to Arthur Butcher in March 1905 until 1911. At this point in time Humphrey Wickham Calcutt became licensee, staying throughout the First World War years until well into the post-war period. Pike's Blue Book of 1910-11 identified H.W. Calcutt as the licensee, and Kelly's Directory of 1927 showed Humphrey Wickham Calcutt at *The Wheatsheaf* public house. The last publican was Robert Evans Mustchin from 1928. When an application for licence renewal with the licensing board of 1932 was refused on the grounds that the premises were unsuitable and the business not viable, it ceased trading and became a private house with the name 'Old Wheatsheaf House' on the front door.

The White Hart, on the east side of Bridge Street, shown on the 1785 town plan alongside the names Benjamin Fugar and Thomas Wakeford, was originally a

42 The White Hart *before its rebuild in the 1880s.*

small stone-walled cottage-like building with two bow windows and a door between with sash windows above and a hipped tiled roof. It was owned by George Constable, whose Swallow Brewery was opposite. It is shown in the early photograph between Bridge House (Herrington's drapery shop) and the 17th-century cottage next to the *General Abercrombie*. Records show Henry Hammond as signing the 1807 petition for reparations. He was followed by James Stallard, as recorded in the 1824 list of licensees. The auction of 1829 described the property as having three bedrooms, a garret, tap room, stables and piggery. Richard Parrish was listed in the 1839 Pigot & Co. directory with the subsequent census records for 1841 and 1851 registering John Boxall as publican at *The White Hart*, this being confirmed by the list of licensees of 1847 and Kelly's Directory of 1855.

The next census year shows Stephen Kinchett registered at *The White Hart*, confirmed in the GPO Directory of 1862. The Arundel Alehouse Licence Book registers Stephen Kingchett as licensee at *The White Hart*, recording his death in 1878, when his widow Jane became licensee until her death in 1883. However, the 1874 GPO Directory lists Jane Kinchett at *The White Hart*, with the 1881 census registering her not only as publican but also blind. Her daughter Ellen, living with her at the time, would no doubt have assisted her mother in running the alehouse. She took over as joint licensee with John Forrester Hall from 14 January 1884. Within a four-month period the licence was transferred to J.F. Hall, as shown on the inn sign, suggesting that Ellen Kinchett was no longer living at *The White Hart*. John Hall then remained as registered licensee for fifteen years, during which time he had married a new woman in his life, Elizabeth, to whom, on his death, the licence was transferred on 6 March 1899.

The 1891 census registers John F. Hall as publican at *The White Hart*, as does the Arundel Directory of 1892, showing him at *The White Hart Inn*. The establishment was advertised in Kimpton's Popular Guide of 1893 as 'White Hart, Arundel No 1 Lodge to the Royal Ancient Order of Buffalos by the

43 The White Hart *inn sign*.

publican J F Hall, Wine & Spirit Merchant with Good Beds & Stabling and Bean Feasts Provided.' The 1891 census records Frank Slaughter as a licensed victualler at *The White Hart*, in harness with Elizabeth Hall as licensee, until November 1901. This was recorded in the Arundel licence book, with the licence being transferred to Frank Slaughter. He remained as publican until the licence was next transferred to Frank Stevens in October 1909, confirmed in Pike's Blue Book of 1910-11 and in Kelly's Directory of 1905 and 1927, when it was called a public house. In June 1928 it reverted to the Slaughter family, with Frank again becoming publican. Frederick William Arlett followed on briefly as licensee until Oliver George Ayling became the next licensee from April 1933, confirmed in Kelly's Directory of 1936. He stayed until halfway through the Second World War. David Pile became licensee in 1942 and stayed on into the post-war years.

It was rebuilt in its present brick style with tile-hung upper floor in the 1880s and is described as having a comfortable main interior with a large central

44 The White Hart *in 1960.*

copper-plated chimney, decorated wall brasses and dark wooden beams. There is also a rear restaurant room and an attractive beer garden to the side. Like so many present-day town pubs, the sign outside advertising food means that catering is as important as selling beer. Now, as the first public house to greet visitors as they walk in from Arundel railway station or from the Lido car park, it can claim to be the only one surviving from the past on the south side of the River Arun, advertising traditional draught ales from Harveys of Lewes, with a responsibility to make them feel really welcome before they reach those remaining few on the north side.

The White Horse/General Abercrombie featured as *The White Horse* on the 1785 plan of Arundel, alongside the names of William Henty and Elizabeth Gilbert, on the site of what has since been known as the *General Abercrombie*, there being no further reference to *The White Horse* on that location. Records show an early 19th-century Henty & Constable alehouse on the east side of Queen Street, facing the Swallow Brewery opposite. It was modernised in 1936 with a new brick-faced frontage around the original building, its character changing with its becoming a free house and popular with young people. Entrance was through the left-hand door and corridor, off which the public bar was located, together with the catering facilities advertised on the awnings over the windows for morning coffee, luncheons and a buffet bar. There was a large clubroom behind used for different events, one such being the annual reunion of Arundel Scout Groups.

The reason for choosing such a name for an alehouse has not been recorded but, during the mid-18th century, General James Abercrombie was Commander-in-Chief in North America and would no doubt have been regarded with some esteem and significance during the French and Indian war, when the French were our sworn enemies in Europe. He was a genius at organisation,

45 General Abercrombie *before its rebuild.*

46 General Abercrombie *before its demolition*.

managing to assemble 15,000 troops and move them and their supplies through the wilderness, leading an expedition against Fort Carillon. Regrettably his vacillation as a leader (his troops called him 'Mrs Nanny Crombie') resulted in heavy casualties from a disastrous frontal attack on a fortified French position without the benefit of artillery support in 1759. He was immediately recalled to England. His name is remembered for a different reason in Arundel, when the building bearing it was burnt down in 1993 and replaced with a mews housing development commemorating the name 'Abercrombie'.

An advertisement in Kimpton's Guide of 1893 featured a picture of a yacht at sea and showed the *General Abercrombie*'s connection with the boatmen of the Buller family by emphasising that there were 'Boats on Hire for pleasure of fishing with live bait supplied from orders received at the Old Bridge House', now demolished but remembered as 'Buller's'. In addition, the advertisement promoted their supplying of bean feasts, a popular service of the time by employers, who provided their employees with an annual celebration dinner at which beans and bacon were regarded as the indispensable dish.

George Street was the licensee in 1824, confirmed in the 1829 auction, which detailed the property as having three bedrooms, two sitting rooms, a garret and a soldiers' room. He was followed by John Boxall, as recorded in Pigot's Directory of 1839. Thomas Smith featured in the General Post Office Directory of 1845, followed by John Richards in the Kelly's Directory of 1855 and the GPO Directory of 1862. The 1861 census confirmed that, by this time, John Richards was fifty-seven years of age. He was registered as licensee in 1863 in Arundel Alehouse Licence Book. John Thomas Slatter followed as licensee in 1870 until 1873, when Edward Slaughter took over as publican in April. The 'Slatter' and 'Slaughter' spellings stem from early verbal census returns, an anomaly that the family's research corroborates, though direct relationship between John Thomas and Edward has not been established.

47   The New Inn at Crossbush.

The 1871 census recorded that Richard Slaughter was a cooper, shown as such in the GPO 1874 Directory, probably working for the family. Mr E. Slaughter was named as being at the *General Abercrombie* in both the Arundel Directory of 1892 and the 1891 census. Edward Slaughter stayed on as innkeeper until 1899, with the licence book records showing his death in May 1900. His widow Ellen (*née* Ayling) then became licensee in June 1901 until 1922. This was recorded in Pike's Blue Book of 1910-11, the Pigot's Directory of 1911 and the Licensing Minute Book of 1916-35.

The next licensee was Frederick (Nip) Slaughter, who took over in February 1922. He was the youngest of Ellen's eleven children, staying as publican until 1960 when his wife Sylvia Frances, then in her late sixties, took over as licensee for two years. Sylvia was the daughter of William Jupp Slaughter (1868-1925), who was the son of boatman James of *The Hare and Hounds*, the eldest son of the nine children of John Slaughter, and brother to Edward. Family records show that Sylvia and her brother William James were born at *The New Inn* in the village of Crossbush, near Arundel, where their father and mother Annie (*née* Simpson) were publicans. When William Jupp Slaughter died, the beerhouse at Crossbush had become known as *The Plough and Sail*, retaining this name until converted into a private residence. While at the *General Abercrombie* Sylvia had looked after her brother and, when she retired as publican, they went to live in a house in Ford Road. She continued to look after him until his death in 1977, surviving him until her death at ninety-two in 1986.

Florence (Flo) May Pecksen became licensee in April 1962 and was followed in October 1963 by Leslie Hugh Fletcher. Tom Pook and then Bob Belden were the last publicans before the premises burnt down.

VI

Premises without Licence Records

The Bear or ***The Black Bull*** was reputed to be in Maltravers Street, now on the corner of The Cut, described as early or mid-18th-century but shown on the 1785 town plan, suggesting that its history went back earlier than its present-day appearance. Today, it has red brick with grey headers in Flemish bond with a hip-tiled roof, a catslide to the north, a west gable, and is tile hung. It comprises two storeys with a plain stringcourse of grey headers above a ground floor, three double-hung sash windows at the first floor and two segment-headed at the ground floor. Up six brick steps with ashlar treads is a 19th-century door in segment headed frame, with a cellar door under the east ground-floor window.

Identification of Arundel inn names was helped by the issue of 17th-century tokens. Through these, *The Bear* was linked with the name of James Carter in 1658 and the *George and Dragon* with Joseph Russell. The latter token shows St George fighting the dragon. The words 'JOSEPH RUSSELL AT THE' surround the image on the obverse, 'ARUNDELL IN SUSSEX' is on the reverse and 'HIS HALF PENY' written in the centre. It is assumed that the present *George and Dragon* at Houghton, as part of Arundel, is the one shown on the map of Sussex taverns in John Taylor's book printed in London in 1636. This included 'a Relation of the Wine Tavernes' on its title page. Both Arundel and Houghton were shown in the catalogue of taverns in Taylor's book. Property leases granted by Arundel Corporation identifies an indenture dated 1695, by which the mayor and burgesses let to George Moore 'their tenement or shopp lyinge between the Butchers Shambles and the inn bearing the sign of *The Black Bull*', thus locating a beerhouse in Old Market Street. This was probably the one previously named *The Bear*, as recorded by G.W. Eustace in his book on Arundel.

It would appear that *The Bear* or *The Black Bull* did exist prior to the 1785 map of Arundel, but was no longer shown as functioning as an approved tavern at the time of the map itself. Though the present house is designated early 18th-century and not 17th-century, further research has shown that there was

48 *Site of* The Bear *or* The Black Bull.

an earlier timber-framed building on the site. Its external asymmetry, with a massive chimney at its west end by the hipped roof and a corner that converges towards the rear, suggests that there was an earlier building, larger than the present. Further investigation within the building itself shows a huge double-backed Tudor brick fireplace between what should be rooms of equal size, the right-hand one being square as expected but the left-hand one wedge-shaped, converging towards the rear and considerably smaller. In the nearside corner of this room a floor hatch gives way to a large cellar that extends below ground level to beyond the line of the outside wall, showing where the earlier building was aligned. Accountable for the asymmetry is the realignment of the London road at the beginning of the 19th century, requiring space occupied by that end of the house to allow insertion of The Cut and the creation of the triangulation needed to smooth traffic flow to the new castle lodge being built.

Records show that the house was once owned by the Duke of Norfolk and it was damaged during the bombardment of the castle by Cromwellian forces during the Civil War. It was rebuilt in its early 18th-century style over a period of time. It was reputed to have had a secret tunnel leading from the castle as a potential escape route in emergencies.

The **George**, located at the top end of the High Street on the right, was reputed to have existed in 1570, though its present façade suggests that it was rebuilt in the mid-18th century in typical Georgian style, red brick with characteristic arched fanlight-type windows and pitched tile roof masked by a parapet. Castle archives, based on parchment indentures, show that Justinian Chandler sold the inn in 1649 to Nethaniah Older, who in 1664 leased it to William Knight, a vintner, who survived only four years. His widow Ann Knight took over and transferred the lease of the 'little stable, the long stable, the grand parlour, the Star chamber, the George chamber, the Rose and the Crown' to Charles Verrall. He in 1765 leased it to George Blanch. By 1779 Sir John Shelley had sold the property to Blanch. The 1785 town plan confirms this, showing the name of George Blanch alongside the site of the inn itself. George Blanch was famed

49 *Site of the* George.

for the meals and entertainment demanded by the rival political parties of Sir John Shelley and the Duke of Norfolk, the *George* being used by the Dukes of Norfolk until superseded by the *Norfolk Arms*.

With George Blanch in charge of these extravagant dinners, held annually in August with the gift of a buck from the Lord of the Manor to the mayor and corporation, the cost of such an extravaganza was typical of the times. For example, as described by G.W. Eustace in his history of Arundel and the castle, the 'Buckfeast' bill for 31 August 1779 of £9 1s. 5d. presented to the mayor, Mr John Holmes, included a mere £2 2s. 0d. for dinners alone. The balance was devoted to punch, port, madeira, beer and negus, a hot sweetened wine with water named after Colonel F. Negus, its inventor, who died in 1732.

The *George* survived as a residence with provision for shops following the demolition of many houses at the top end of High Market Street (as the High Street was then called) with the enclosing of land to the Norfolk estates and the extension of the castle walls below the West Gate. This began during the period 1802 to 1815 and when Charles (11th Duke of Norfolk) died the work was continued by his successors. A notable find on the premises, during restoration in the latter part of the 20th century, was that of a hidden cupboard, behind which was a door into a lost room containing a monk's vestment draped over a chair. The old coach inn is now the repository of an extensive antiques showroom and smaller shops.

50   *Site of* The Orchard.

The Orchard is a name that has not been corroborated authentically in any discovered documentation. However, in the extension to Farmers Lane on the 1785 town plan there were only two residents shown on the left-hand side going down to the river. They were Richard Clear and Richard Emery, in what are described as 18th-century terraced cottages of red brick with grey headers and a pitched tile roof, with brick parapets to the gable ends and eaves cornice with *cyma reversa* modillions. The first-floor stringcourse and voussoirs are of gauged and rubbed red brick. Although there are now two doors with ashlar steps to each, there is a blocked window over the doors and trapdoors each to cellarage. The window to the left is a canted bay shop window with glazing bars and moulded cornice. Behind the cottages was an extensive pear orchard with a footpath leading down to Ship Yard (now River Road).

The discovery of five old coins and tokens lying on the rubble of the old cellars, during renewal of rotten timber flooring, dated the cottages as mid- or early 18th-century. This find comprised a William and Mary halfpenny of 1694, a John Wilkinson Iron Master token from 1787, a George III cartwheel penny of 1797, a Portuguese coin of 1799 inscribed 'Maria I dei Gratia' and 'Portugaliae et Algarbiorum Regina', and a Wellington commemorative medallion with 1814 on the obverse and 1816 on the reverse. The William and Mary coin was in quite good condition, suggesting that it was unlikely to have been in circulation long before rolling through a gap in the floorboards, thus giving credence to its dating. George III cartwheel pennies were struck only in 1797 and then withdrawn in 1816, due to the rise in the price of copper following the flagrant practice at the time of melting down the coins and selling them on to copper dealers at inflated prices. By an Act of Parliament of July 1817, any coin or token so dated was declared illegal after 1 January 1818. The era of commercial coins was over and the government and the sovereign exercised their prerogative from 1821 to provide adequate supplies of regal copper coinage.

The medallion with the legend 'WELLINGTON & VICTORY', commemorating the successful Peninsular Campaign against the French, was clearly marked in its exergue with 1814. Since literacy was minimal in those days, and the obverse clearly showed the recognisable side-view head of the Duke of Wellington, it would be acceptable as currency or even as a coin of the realm, especially with its having an unworn thread-milled edge, not rack-milled as on silver coins, and being complete in itself.

Further research, however, identified that this was one minted for the Irish market, showing on the reverse as it did Hibernia (resembling Britannia as portrayed in currency of the period) seated on a rock facing to the left, holding an olive branch in her outstretched right hand and supporting a spear in the crook of her left arm. By her side is an oval shield bearing the Arms of Ireland, an Irish harp, and on the left is a distant view of a three-masted ship. The legend around the periphery is 'EDW^d BEWLEY' with 1816 in the exergue. Research has confirmed that Edward Bewley was a greengrocer, and later a tea and coffee importer, at 35 South Earl Street, Dublin.

For such a medallion to be found in Arundel, it was likely to have been brought to the house by a sailor returning from coastwise shipping or a soldier back from the wars. However, it was the presence of the Portuguese coin that gave proof that this had been brought into the house by a seagoing sailor or by a soldier returning from the Peninsular War.

The John Wilkinson token, minted for payment to workers in the iron trade and in excellent condition, with a fine picture of a drop hammer on the reverse, would have come from another source. It was likely to have been brought in by a visitor from the Midlands or further west from Shropshire or Wales, where copper and iron foundries existed. The spread of such 'tokens' gives credence to the belief that the two cottages together, with their proximity to the river and the doss houses and brothels of Ship Yard, could well have been a beerhouse, particularly as it appears to have pre-dated the later riverbank beerhouse *The Jolly Sailors*. Another piece of evidence was the discovery of two old Constable Brewery signs among the cellar rubble during later refurbishment.

Since most beerhouses were known by a location name giving some indication of their function, this

51 *Old coins and tokens* (The Orchard).

had to be established next. The property was part of a large orchard, as shown on the 1785 town plan. This was confirmed by an eye-witness report from a resident born in the area in 1920, who spoke of the owners as Mr and Mrs Hulls, and on a conveyance document dated 1926 assigning the property to William Hulls. It is conceivable that the early users of such a beerhouse, referring to it by its location, would call it '*The Orchard*'. Current hearsay from a number of individual sources has, in fact, given credibility to this name, though no primary source documents have been found to corroborate this fact. One early owner was reported as saying that there was an inn sign found among the rubble that went to a public house on the south coast that collected such memorabilia, but this fact has not been corroborated to date, nor has the inn sign itself been located.

The Starr, described as a 'Common Inne', was identified in a parchment indenture dated 4 April 1676 relating to a sale of property located at the top of High Market Street. The document was between residents of Arundel named as Christopher Elliott, tallow chandler, Robert Booker, tallow chandler, and John Westwood, barber, and the properties described as:

> All that messuage or tenement backside and garden thereunto belonging with the appurtenances situate lyeing and being in the High Market Street in the Borough of Arundell aforesaid now in the tenure or occupation of Thomas Drewett ... adjoining to the backside and garden late of one Henry Bull and now of one Thomas Colebrook on the south east part of the said High Street on or towards the south west, and to the Common Inne called the *Starr* on the north west part and the Castle Ditch on the north east part with all commodities ... which said messuage and premises were therefore purchased by the said Christopher Elliott from John Goldwire of Arundell.

Tokens dated 1657, 1666 and 1667 have been linked to Thomas Drewett, trading as tallow chandler. Of the other names included in this indenture, the 1785 plan of Arundel shows Charles Elliott living on the left-hand side of the High Street, William Booker on the right-hand side of Tarrant Street where the old candle factory was sited, and John Booker in Old Market Street not far from John Bull, at the large property on the corner of the lane down to the *Kings Arms*. All these buildings at the top end of the High Street were demolished during the years after 1800 by Duke Charles and his descendants in order to incorporate them and their gardens, which ran up to the castle ditch, into the castle grounds. The London road was diverted in 1803 to run south of St Nicholas' Church, and the old castle gate north-east of the churchyard removed and a new one built further south on the site of the present lodge. This demolition covered buildings opposite and would have included *The Starr Inne*.

However, the name 'Star' was retained. The reasoning was attributed to the magnificent mansion built during the early 15th century in Tarrant Street, with access through a walled pleasure garden lying between the house and the river, for the use of John Fitzalan, Lord Maltravers, and his family. His continuous dispute with the Duke of Norfolk over ownership of the castle would have rendered him otherwise without a residence. Within a short time the house had degenerated into a hostelry, known as the *Star*, and was later converted into tenements for labourers until its demolition in 1833. Its grandeur was remembered by a resident writing her memoirs in 1907, describing how at the end of a long passage stood a large dilapidated building called The Old Nineveh that, in former years, must have been a place of note. By then it had only a few rooms left fit for habitation. These had been let to three separate families at a low rent and the writer was astonished, when calling there on a business matter, to see the wide staircase, balustrade and pillars, in handsome oak and still retaining a highly polished finish, while so much of the building was in decay.

52 *Former Congregational Church.*

When it was pulled down to make way for the Roman Catholic Trinity Chapel (later a Congregational Chapel), of an architectural style hardly matching the beauty of its predecessor, gone forever was workmanship of such quality and elegance. Though grand in proportions, the Old Nineveh's entrance hall was eclipsed in appearance by the superbly carved staircase with its oak balusters and the upper flights shaped as Janus-faced figures. The handrails were moulded and the newel posts at the bottom of each flight decorated with carved heads and drops. The principal room was described by earlier writers, particularly by G.W. Eustace in his book on Arundel, as of stately proportions with lofty ceiling, walls wainscoted in moulded dark-framed oak panels and a large open fireplace with chimneypiece of polished Sussex marble. An elaborately carved mantelpiece was surmounted by a wrought framework, displaying a trellis pattern of leaves and flowers. About its centre was carved in bold relief a horse with an oak branch in its mouth, the recognised emblem of the Earls of Arundel.

With the loss of the old house, the Victorian chapel is now utilised as a multi-stalled antiques market, with a display board still showing the site as Nineveh House.

53 *Nineveh House Antiques Centre.*

54 Site of The Sundial.

The Sundial was shown on the 1785 map at the junction of Short Lane (now Bakers Arms Hill) and Old Market Street (now Maltravers Street). The cottage on the corner, now known colloquially as the Little House but named 'Bakers Arms Cottage', shows Martin as the householder, next to a property marked with the name *The Sundial*. In the Department of the Environment's list of buildings of special architectural or historic interest it is described as a row of 17th-century cottages of red brick grey headers, Flemish bond with a pitched tile roof. Behind is an extensive catslide clay-tiled roof covering expansive cellarage (the width of two cottages), with access from the front for delivering casks. Inside, the ceilings are head-height timbered, while at the rear a magnificent Tudor fireplace occupies almost the full width of the wall of one cottage. Reference documents show mortgage details dated 1768 and further reference is made to a mortgage discharge of £1,000 for a thousand years in Old Market Street, Arundel, dated 14 March 1779, with John Macklin's name. Since John Macklin also appears in the Universal British Directory of 1793-8, recorded as a victualler, it presupposes that he could have been associated with the running of *The Sundial*. On the façade brickwork is the mark 'WILL POWELL 179★', the final digit being unclear. Research by an owner suggests that at one time there was direct access between the corner cottage and the adjacent right-hand pair in Old Market Street to an apple orchard behind with its cider house. The *Bakers Arms'* licensee, in the premises round the corner, could have exploited this facility too, as a way to deliver beer casks to the beerhouse. To date, no reference documents have been found or street directory records to show any further alehouse or beerhouse evidence for *The Sundial*.

VII

Conclusion

Although research has uncovered many unexpected gems among photographic records to stimulate nostalgic memories of old times, including a few of the publicans themselves, what the reader must not forget are the records of achievement of the men and women who had managed these establishments.

Research into the licensing records has shown the dominant families and a number of remarkable widows who managed so successfully the inns and taverns in Arundel during the past two hundred years. The word remarkable, justifying their immortality, has been used to describe these women when they reigned supreme, particularly in an era when men were regarded as superior and women subservient. Many would have been supported by their sons and daughters acting as assistant innkeepers.

Early evidence is sparse and what has been found details the women born in the late 18th and early 19th centuries who took charge of the beer-drinking places during the turbulent days of wars with the French, the beginning of the Industrial Revolution and the birth of the British Empire. Demands on the labour force of the nation were not just satisfied by men, but by women and children too. Many widows lived to a ripe old age and died in harness, serving beer until they dropped, one such being Sarah Roe at *The Hare and Hounds* for twenty years and another being Elizabeth Overington at *The Old Ship* for twenty-four years.

Frances Booker was a licensee for twenty-nine years, spanning the First World War. Mary Ann Hulls was the longest-serving licensee, going through forty years and both World Wars, but one of the saddest was Jane Kinchett, who died when only fifty-five. She was registered blind for nine years while licensee at *The White Hart* and was supported by her unmarried daughter Ellen. Two of the eldest survivors were Sylvia Slaughter who, after widowhood at the *General Abercrombie*, lived to the grand old age of ninety-two, and Mary Jones, who ran the *Victory* until well into her seventies and lived as the longest-serving ex-publican until aged over eighty-three.

The demands made during the two World Wars of the 20th century, when the menfolk went off to serve their country, many never to return, showed what these women could do in overcoming food shortages, experiencing air raids and still giving a superlative service to their customers. The family names that stand out as part of the Arundel heritage include the Bookers and the Burrells at the *Newburgh Arms*, the Ellwoods at *The Swan*, the Hares at the *Norfolk Arms*, the Hulls at *The Jolly Sailors* and *The Heart in Hand*, the Slaughters at *The Hare and Hounds*, *The Ship and Lighter* and the *General Abercrombie*, and the Wakefords at the *Queens Arms*.

Index of Arundel Ale and Beerhouses

Figures in bold refer to illustrations.

Alehouses

The Black Rabbit, 14, 15, 20, 48-9, **48**,
Crown, 5, 6, 8, 12, 14-16, 43, 49-52, **50**, 63, 64, 66
The Dolphin/The Bridge Hotel, 5, 12, 13-18, 45, 52-5, **54**
The Eagle, 8, 13, 19, 21, 23, 55-9, **56**
Kings Arms, 5-6, 12, 14-18, 20, 39-41, **40**, 46, 82
The Milehouse/The White Swan, 18, 20, 56-9, **57**, **58**
Newburgh Arms, viii, 12, 14-15, 17-18, 41-3, **43**, 46, 53, 86
Norfolk Arms, viii, 6, 12, 14-15, 18, 20, 43-6, **44**, 50-2, 79, 86
The Old Ship, vii, viii, 12, 14-16, 18-19, 33-4, 59-60, **60**
The Railway Inn, viii, 18, 20, 60-3, **62-3**
The Red Lion, viii, 8, 12, 14-18, 20, 50, 63-6, **65-6**
The St Mary's Gate Inn, 6, 12, 14, 16, 18, 20, 34-5, 46-8, **47**
The Swan Hotel, 19, 20, **58**, 59, 70
The Wheatsheaf, 12-15, 17-18, 22, 70-1, **70-1**
The White Hart, 5, 12, 14-16, 18, 20, 71-4, **72-3**, 85
The White Horse/General Abercrombie, 5, 7, 12, 16, 18, 36-8, **37**

Beerhouses

Bakers Arms, viii, 16, 17, 21-2, **22**, 26, 84
Brewers Arms, 17, 20, 22-3, 55

The Hare and Hounds, 17, 25-6, **26**, 76, 85-6
The Heart in Hand, vii, 8, 16, 18-19, 26-7, **27**, 29, 63, 86
The Jolly Sailors, vii, viii, 6, 14, 16-19, 27-31, **28**, 81, 86
Queens Arms, 16-18, 22, 24-5, **24-5**, 86
The Ship and Lighter, vii, viii, 16, 19, 31-3, **32**, 86
The Victory, viii, 16, 18-19, 33-6, **33-4**, **36**
The White Horse, 5, 7, 12, 16, 18, 36-7, **36**, 39, 67, 74

Premises without Licence Records

The Bear/The Black Bull, 77-8, **78**
The Bell/The Blue Bell, 6, 7
Bricklayers Arms, 17
Carpenters Arms, 17
The Chestnut, 17
George, 5, 6, 42, 51, 79, **79**
The Mount Pleasant, 17
The Orchard, 30, 80, **80-1**, 82
The Red Lion and Anchor, 7, 8, 63
The Ship, 6, 13, 18, 45, 59
The Spread Eagle, 7
The Starr, 7, 37, 82
The Sundial, 6, 13-14, 84, **84**
The Three Mariners, 7, 8
The Yew Tree, 17

Index of Publican Families

AYLING
  Ellen, 76
  Oliver George, 73
BALCHIN
  William, 12, 15, 43, 50
BARKSHIRE
  Charles, 45
BARRY
  Maureen, viii, 43
  Robert Edward James, 43
BEHRENS
  Otto John Henry, 23, 49, 55
BISHOP(P)
  Edward, 12, 39
BLANCH(E)
  George, 6, 14, 43, 49, 63, 78-9
BOOKER
  Frances, 18, 42, 85-6
  Thomas, 42
BOSWORTH
  George, 64
  May Charlotte, 64
BOXALL
  John, 14, 72, 75
BURCHELL
  John, 16
BURRELL
  Arthur, 52
  Charlotte, 42
  Lewis Gordon, 52
  Mary Ann, 53
  William Lewis, 17, 42

BURTON
  John, 17, 22, **23**, 55
  Sarah, 22-3
CALCUTT
  Humphrey Wickham, 18, 71
  Humphrey William, 22, 64, 68
COLLINS
  James, 34
  Susan Emily, 35
  William James, 34-5
CONSTABLE
  George, 9, 14, 19, 31, 59, 72
COOPER
  Sarah, 45
  Thomas, 45
CORBETT
  William, 17, 39
COX
  Charles Owen, 43
  Joyce, 43
DAUGHTREY
  James, 17, 21
  Jane, 21
DENYER
  Bernie, 43
  Maureen, 43
ELLIOTT
  Edward, 12, 14-15, 59
  John, 12, 38
ELLWOOD
  Elizabeth, 67
  John, 64, 67
  Mary Jane, 64, 67

ELSTON
  Annie, 61
  Henry Edward, 61
FARR
  John, 19, 60
  Kathleen, 60
FORREST
  Edmund, 16, 52
  Rhoda, 16
FOX
  Brian, 35
GARWOOD
  Robert, 45
GILBERT
  John, 7, 8, 63
  Elizabeth, 7, 8, 74
GLOSSOP
  Alfred Joseph, 47
  Elizabeth, 15, 46
  George, 21
  Robert, 12, 46
  Thomas Phillip, 22
  William Edward, 18, 59
GREENFIELD
  Edward James, 31
  Tom, 27
HAINES
  David, 61
  Sue, 61
HALL
  Elizabeth, 72-3
  John, 72
HANSON
  Derek, viii, 66
  Sara, 66

HARE
  Elizabeth Ann, 18
  George William Favonious, 45
  John Nibloe, 45
  Neil, viii, 46
HATCHER
  Charles, 27, 39
HEATER
  James, 38
HERSEE
  Alfred James, 47
  Caroline, 14, 16-17, 39
  Ernest Alfred George, 18, 47
  George, 16, 47
  Jane, 61
  John, 12, 15, 70
HINSON
  Andrew, 47
  Elizabeth, 47
HULLS
  Agnes, 29
  Alfred, 16, 27
  Ellen, 29
  Ernest George, 18-19, 29
  Mary Ann, 18, 27, 85
  Richard, 16, 29-30
  Richard William, 30
  William, 30, 35, 82
JEX
  Anita, 69
  Anthony Allan John, 69

JOEL
  Charles, 35
  Maimie, 35
  Paula, 35
JONES
  James, 33
  Mary, 85
JUPP
  Archie, 55, 57
  Fanny, 18
  Frances, 26, 57
  Joseph, 57
KINCHETT
  Ellen, 18, 72, 85
  Jane, 72, 85
  Stephen, 72
KINCHITT
  Stephen, 16
KNIGHT
  Albert, 43
  Ann, 78
  Henry Charles, 25, 49
  June, viii, 43
  Sam, 49
  William, 78
LANCASTER
  John, 17
  Sarah, 17
LEE
  William John, 31
LINDSEY
  Elisabeth, 61
  Jim, 61
LOCK
  Edward Thomas, 42
  Jessie, 42
LUCAS
  Fred, 17, 71
  William, 6, 14, 67
MACKLIN
  John, 14, 84
MARTIN
  Alice Emma, 56
  Eileen, 43
  Francis Esther, 55, 56
  John, 43
  Percy Edgar, 56
  Roger George, 55
MONK
  Eliza, 21
  William, 16, 21-2
MORLEY
  Mary, 14
  William, 16, 63
MUSTCHIN
  Ellen Kate, 53
  Ernest Frank, 47, 53
  Robert Evans, 71
ODDE
  Gemma, viii, 36
  Ian, viii, 34, 36
OLIVER
  John, 48
  James, 14, 49
OSBORNE
  Frank, 53
  Mary, 53
OVERINGTON
  Edward, 16, 59
  Elizabeth, 16, 85
  Owen, 38
PARRISH
  Richard, 15, 63, 72
PARSONS
  Arthur George, 18, 38
PEAKE
  Edward Charles, 18, 61
  Tabitha Ellen, 61
PHILLIPS
  Joseph, 33-4
POAT
  Emma, 59
  Walter, 59
PUTTOCK
  Archibald Albert Francis, 42
  Edward, 8, 49, 59
  George, 8-9, 13-14, 22, 70
QUAIFE
  William, 44-6
RANDALL
  Henry, 16, 50, 62, 64
  Jane, 50
REDMAN
  George, 27, 39
RIDDLE
  George, 38
ROE
  Charles, 25
  Sarah, 17, 25, 85
ROWSELL
  Diana, 70
  Ken, 70
SEARLE
  Elizabeth, 16, 59
  John, 14, 16, 59
SERMON
  Caroline, 27
  James Henry, 27
  William, 16, 27
SHARP
  William, 16, 18, 33
SILVERLOCK
  Florence Winifred, 40
  Frank Edward, 40
  Victor William John, 40
SLATTER
  John Thomas, 38, 49, 75
SLAUGHTER
  Edward, 18, 75-6
  Ellen, 18, 76
  Frances Jupp, 26
  Frank, 16, 38, 73
  Frederick, 64
  George Edward, 23
  James, 16, 26
  John William, 16, 31, 76
  May Charlotte, 64
  Richard, 76
  Sylvia Frances, vii, 76, 85
  William James, 76
  William Jupp, 16, 22, 26, 76
SPEARMAN
  Alan, 60
  Mary, 60
STALLARD
  Edward, 12, 52
  James, 15, 72
STEVENS
  Frank, 18, 73
  James, 64, 67
  Mary Jane, 18, 67-8
STREET
  Ernie, 35, 59
  Flora, 59
  George, 15, 75
  William, 15, 39
STRUDWICK
  Thomas, 39
STURT
  Fanny, 22
  Henry, 22
TEE
  Archie George, 47
  Lilly Ann, 61
  Thomas, 61
  William Granger, 61
TILLEY
  Annie, 52
  George, 52
WAKEFORD
  Eliza, 24-5
  Louisa, 24
  Thomas, 5, 16, 18
  William, 17, 24, 71
WATTS
  William, 16, 50
WILTSHIRE
  Iris, 60
  James, 60
WITHALL
  Lillian, 69
  William Jason, 68-9
WITHAM
  Edward, 17, 64
  Lucy, 64
  Thomas, 64